LEAVING ACADEMIA

LEAVING ACADEMIA

Ditch the blanket, take the skills

Dr Emma Williams

First published in 2024 by Intellectual Perspective Press
© Copyright Dr Emma Williams.

All rights reserved. No part of this publication may be reproduced, stored in or introduced into a retrieval system, or transmitted, in any form, or by any means (electronic, mechanical, photocopying, recording or otherwise) without the prior written permission of the publisher.

The right of Dr Emma Williams to be identified as the author of this work has been asserted in accordance with the Copyright, Designs and Patents Act 1988.

This book is sold subject to the condition that it shall not, by way of trade or otherwise, be lent, resold, hired out, or otherwise circulated without the publisher's prior consent in any form of binding or cover other than that in which it is published and without a similar condition including this condition being imposed on the subsequent purchaser.

To find out more about our authors and books visit:
www.intellectualperspective.com

CONTENTS

Praise for Leaving Academia x
Free for you xii

Are you my "one reader"? xiv
   How to get the most from this book xvii

SECTION ONE: So, how is postdoc life treating you?. . .1
   Chapter 1: Have you hit peak postdoc? 3
      Are you sitting in academia's shadow? 5
      Peak, Plateau or Plummet? 10
      Peak Postdoc 12
      Postdoc Plateau 13
      Postdoc Plummet 13
   Chapter 2: Shrugging off the academic comfort
      blanket 15
      The itchy scratchy comfort blanket 16
      The twilight zone (fears of the unknown) 18
      That sinking feeling (sunk cost fallacy). 20

The anti-Terminator clause (I can't come back) . . 22

I am who I am (vocation). 26

Your PI doesn't have the answer
   (asking the wrong people) 27

SECTION TWO: Unravel the blanket and build a net: getting ready to move on 33

Chapter 3: Pull yourself together: threads of gold,
   steel and purple 37

   The golden thread (your values) 38

   The steel thread (your strengths) 40

   The purple thread (your courage) 43

Chapter 4: Dealing with others: the good,
   the bad and the … 49

   Asking for help 50

   Curating your network 53

   Difficult conversations 58

   The net we weave 61

Chapter 5: Building your toolkit 63

   It's a job to get a job .63

   Stop looking like a postdoc 66

   Salary is a lonely word. 68

SECTION THREE: So, you've got your new role. What's next? 71

Chapter 6: Let's not make another blanket 74

The day one question 76
Another thread (the tripwire) 77
You're not a cat. Be curious. 80
Chapter 7: Peak to peak: the next career steps 85
One to many: building your career a
peak at a time 86
Stay connected. Not tethered 91

Conclusion: Prove it's possible 97
Me? A mentor? 98
About the author 100
Acknowledgements 103
More Praise for Leaving Academia 106

PRAISE FOR LEAVING ACADEMIA

This is a must-read for all academics, whether or not you have ever wondered about careers beyond academia. Should be required reading when you start your academic career. As someone who took 10 years wondering whether to leave academia (and then ultimately doing so) much of this book deeply resonated with me and I wish I had read it sooner.

Dr Michele Veldsman,
Director of Neuroscience, Cambridge Cognition

But here's the kicker: Emma gets us. Like, really gets us. Her nerdy references alone show me that she speaks our language and it works because her advice then cuts straight through into me. And let's not forget the constant pep talks reminding us just how smart we are. It's like having a cheerleader in book form!

Amy Gaskin, Bioinformatician,
Public Health Wales NHS Trust

This book is very good food for thought. At points it felt as though the author was reading my mind and thought process! Which makes you realise what a common experience we are all having. A great starting place to get into the right mindset to begin the process of exploring different career options.

Dr Hannah Jones, Postdoc,
University of Oxford

Reading Emma's Leaving Academia is like meeting an old friend over a cup of coffee and chatting about your career options. It's so refreshing. I believe everybody will find their chapter in this book.

Dr Hana Mlčochová ,
Strategic Engagement Manager, UKRI

How I wish this book was available when I was going through the motions of leaving academia! Emma's writing flows and the book is clear, encouraging and practical.

Dr Lucia Carassiti,
Project Manager, JLR

Dr. Emma Williams' "Leaving Academia: ditch the blanket, take the skills" isn't your typical career guide. It's a supportive companion, hand-in-hand with you as you navigate the emotions and practicalities of a transition from postdoc to a fulfilling career beyond academia.

Dr Chris Jeffs, Careers Adviser,
Oxford University Careers Service

The fruit of 20 years coaching post-docs, Dr Emma Williams offers a quick read but long ponder. I most appreciate how she fires courage, gently weaving escape threads, to enable gifted post-docs to fly the academic nest and find their God-given vocation.

Rt Revd Dr Jill Duff, Anglican Bishop of Lancaster
(the first scientist I met in Cambridge)

FREE FOR YOU

Read

This book is designed to get you thinking about whether leaving academia is right for you and, if it is, we will explore how to move on successfully. It is also designed to be brief and pack a (gentle) punch. I know how busy a postdoc's life is!

Think

Every career decision needs some good thinking behind it. I include exercises in the text to get you started. I didn't have room for all of them and so I have created a resource bank with some extra bonuses to get you using your greatest resource: that postdoc brain of yours.

Do

Once you have decided to move on, then I know you will want to crack on with the practicalities. Where do I look for jobs? How do I build a great CV? How do I prepare for an interview? This book would need to be in the weight-lifting section if I included it all. So, I have created the Leaving Academia Toolkit to help you. Time to showcase that marvellous you to the outside world.

Click

All this, my postdoc friend, is a click away at www.thenerdcoach/leaving_academia

ARE YOU MY "ONE READER"?

It seems daft to have written a book for just one person. But I had the very good advice to visualise one person who needed this book and write it for them. Not just an avatar but a real live, living, breathing person. This book is written for Sam (an alias because all superheroes have them). Sam was a postdoc. Sam had realised that academia was not their future path. Sam was finding it a tough decision to navigate.

I know there are more Sams out there. In my thirty plus years in and around higher education and research, I have met hundreds of Sams. The postdoc stage is where we gain understanding of being a researcher professionally, having left our student selves behind. Academia will have given us many opportunities, experiences and skills. This stage is exciting because we learn so much about ourselves. I certainly did and that set me on a road to supporting researchers through training, coaching and writing.

All books need a cover, but I was almost tempted with the literary equivalent of an anonymous brown paper bag for this book. That way you could pick it up and read it without anyone knowing you were turning to the dark side![1] But that is what e-readers are great for! I want you to explore your career choices. As a postdoc you have more than you think.

This book is not about academic bashing – an academic career can be a great one. I have worked with postdocs who have gained fellowships and lectureships. They enjoy their careers. This book will have done a great job if you were thinking of leaving but have now made an active and deliberate choice to stay!

But the numbers of permanent academic positions, lifestyle and environment just don't add up for everyone. Sam felt it was time to leave because academia just wasn't meeting their needs anymore. They had glimpsed a better scenario whilst on a project. But Sam was still tied to academia in positive and negative ways. They were wrapped snugly in the academic comfort blanket. It had started to itch. I will introduce you to your purple thread – one of dignity and respect for ourselves. Our careers should demand our respect. It is okay to choose a career that works for us. We can ditch the blanket and embrace the marvellous skills and experiences that academia has given us and share them with a wider world.

I hold two things as true in my work with postdocs:

A postdoc is a super numerate, super literate, problem-solving, project-managing warrior and

The world needs postdocs (it really does) in every walk of life

When I started to write this book, it was suggested by my book coach that I entreat my readers to climb the mountain of leaving academia by waving a flag from the highest height. I am certainly waving the flag. This book should take you from thinking about moving through to your next career steps. Is it a mountain? Possibly. But it is often of one of our own making. There are plenty of unknowns – "stuff" weighing us down. Don't panic – we'll break the process down into steps. But even taking one step might feel like a huge uphill effort. I know from experience that postdocs often share their surprise at how easy some steps are.

Postdocs come in all shapes, sizes, disciplines and settings, but when it comes to leaving there are these groups:

- Determined to be an academic, not even looking at anything else.
- Dissatisfied about the unjustness of their postdoc role (fixed term contracts, long working hours) and demanding the system gets fixed.[2]
- I want to do what I'm doing forever, please.
- I am "only" a postdoc and can't do anything else.
- I really want to move out but don't know how.
- I'm out of here.

This book will help you, whichever group you fall into, because the first step in our careers is understanding where we are and what we want. Sound simple? Too often I find postdocs who are:

So busy pushing research boundaries they haven't explored their own.

Hence the blanket in the title. Have we hidden under the itchy, scratchy comfort blanket of academia? Is it dark under there? Is it weighing you down? Can we use the amazing threads of our academic career to weave a new one which evolves along with us?

So, if you are like Sam, welcome! Let's embark on a journey, my wonderful postdoc friend. We will look at leaving academia, get ready to move on if you want to and then look forward as far as we can into that sparkly future. We will follow Sam's story as we develop your own. Sam has moved roles several times as their opportunities expanded from taking that first step out of academia. As Bilbo explains in *The Lord of the Rings* (J. R. R. Tolkien):

> *"It's a dangerous business, Frodo, going out your door. You step onto the road, and if you don't keep your feet, there's no knowing where you might be swept off to."*

How to get the most from this book

I very much want you to think whilst reading this book. It is deliberately short, but I am hoping for quick read, long ponder. You have taken a major first step in picking this book up. Taking time and space to stop and think is all too rare in this busy world. Take this book somewhere you can think freely and uninterrupted. I'd suggest a coffee shop because I love coffee and background chatter helps me think. You do you. That could almost be the synopsis of this book – finding out what is right for you. No one else.

Taking notes along the way will help. Distilling the thoughts chasing around that mega brain of yours into black and white brings clarity. Clarity is also in conversation. As you start to read, think about people in your network who would be brilliant to discuss your ideas with.

I talk about the academic comfort blanket in section one and will use threads as a metaphor. Along the way I will try to lay out a red thread[3] for you to follow:

	Knot to be forgotten!	These are key truths that postdocs need to know
	Action time	Short exercises to get you thinking about your career
	Resources	Head to the online book resources to access the Leaving Academia Toolkit

ENDNOTES

1. A phrase directed at me when I moved into the professional services side of the university.
2. To the extent of going on strike https://www.nature.com/articles/d41586-023-03298-7
3. Theseus followed a red thread to keep him from the Minotaur https://www.greekmyths-greekmythology.com/myth-of-theseus-and-minotaur/

SECTION ONE

SO, HOW IS POSTDOC LIFE TREATING YOU?

"Light and shadow are opposite sides of the same coin. We can illuminate our paths or darken our way. It is a matter of choice."
– Maya Angelou

Every career journey starts from where you are, right now. That much seems obvious but we can be too eager to look forward. Without understanding our current situation, we may well make unwise choices about the future.

Our current situation is built of our job, circumstances and the environment we find ourselves in. Are we still growing ourselves and our CV? Are we happy? Have we stopped and taken a good look at the environment we find ourselves in? Have we tied ourselves down unwittingly?

It is time to stop and smell the coffee. This section is the essential pre-work to the next steps in your career. You need to make time to do some thinking. Go ahead and book it in your diary now. Too often urgent tasks (your PI demanding results or the masters student looking forlorn) wipe out any time for the important ones. You are important. Your career is important.

The only person who is going to prioritise you is you.

But before you embark on exploring your current patch of Planet Postdoc in this section, I would like you to do one more thing.

In the book resources you will find a timeline exercise. This will help you understand more about your route here. Not everyone embarks on a PhD. A select group of those choose a postdoc. Why did you?

> Postdoc A felt stuck. Unhappy in a second postdoc after a good experience in the first. They were contemplating a third postdoc or non-academic jobs. They looked surprised when I asked, "What was great about the first?" Our timelines hold vital clues as to what might work in our future. Not just things to avoid. But things to actively seek in our next steps. What have you really enjoyed? Not just the work but the environment.

CHAPTER 1:
HAVE YOU HIT PEAK POSTDOC?

I can remember the meeting as if it were yesterday even though several years have passed. I was meeting with Sam in one of those random unofficial courtyards that most large universities have. You know the ones: air conditioner vents, metal fire escape ladders, crumbling concrete paths and a couple of temporary buildings that had probably been there at least twenty years. We sat within one of these. A sad room looking out into the London drizzle. My companion's mood matched the scene perfectly: worried, resigned and full of guilt. If you had transplanted us into a gritty 1980s police drama, we wouldn't have looked out of place.

Why the low mood? Sam had decided to leave academia as they had reached a point where it was not delivering the environment they needed to thrive. We were there to work on interview technique, as this bioscientist was off to explore big pharma. Despite being shortlisted for the role, doubts, lingering guilt and uncertainty peppered our practice session. Sam's decision to leave and the process of doing so were a struggle.

To misquote one of my favourite books[1]: "Reader, they got the role." Given I am writing this book for them and the thousands of postdocs like them (or you?), I decided to interview Sam some six years on from that first transition. I asked them the question "What, at that point, were the dreaded 3am thoughts that kept you awake about being a postdoc?" Their answer surprised me given they had decided to leave. "I think at that time I hadn't realised there were things that should have kept me awake." They had felt the need to move on but perhaps not done the big thinking about why. This isn't a problem unique to academia. People can get stuck in any role.

Why did I pick this Cinderella story? Wherever we work we need to frequently take stock of how we feel and why. I have worked with too many postdocs who have just not woken up and smelt the coffee (mine's black, steady on the water) in time to prevent feeling stuck and miserable. This genuinely breaks my heart.

You are too talented to be stuck!

This version of Cinderella is not a fairy story. Rewarding, enjoyable and happy careers are out there for you (we will find out what Sam did next later on). But don't wait for Prince Charming and a bunch of cute animals to save you whilst singing! Your principal investigator isn't your saviour either. You will need to illuminate your own path. As I see it there are two parts to this: understanding your current situation *and* how you feel about it. Neither of these can, nor should, be thought of lightly. So, make yourself a cuppa[2] and take this steady. In our busy lives it can be easy to avoid reflection.

Are you sitting in academia's shadow?

It was only after starting their new role outside academia that Sam realised a host of feelings "immediately dissipated" and uncovered the extent to which they had normalised their situation. Do you recognise any of these from their list?

- Academia had played on their sense of duty
- Academia had played on their love of research
- Academia was "home" and everything else was "foreign"
- They had learnt to put themself last
- They felt indebted to academic research
- They had worked "obscene" hours to help patients for the project to then stall at the translation stage
- Planning a holiday meant "begging" people to look after their experiments
- No one had left their research group – ever
- Becoming a perfectionist, striving to make their work better and better, had crystalised a belief that they couldn't do "stuff"
- Feeling as if they only had the skillset for the role in hand

These are some of the shadows that the academic research environment can cast. These shadows stop you seeing a way forward or even understanding you have other options. Perhaps the ironic thing is that most derive from you, the wonderful postdoc that you are, wanting to do the very best you can to discover and deliver. School teachers experience similar shadow blindness about their careers. Teaching is often referred to as a vocation or calling. Many of the researchers I work with experience a call to investigate, discover and reveal. A skilful vocation leverages your skill set to build a career that serves a larger purpose. Your research brings value to your discipline, your institution and society at large.

You chose academic research for a myriad of great reasons. Stopping to take stock of whether academia is still delivering for you is important. I will encourage you to do this regularly in your career in section three. Given our eyes acclimatise to the light level, how do we know how dark, for us, it really is? Before we ask some big questions, I want to reiterate that people do have successful and happy academic careers.

This book is not about hating academia, but it is about respecting yourself.

Universities have appraisal systems that focus on work skills development (the next section) but I have yet to see a form that asks the simple (but massive) question "Are you happy in your role?"

We therefore need a structure to help us work out where we are at, a light meter if you will. Let's use one of my favourites. Ikigai is a Japanese concept that combines the two words "iki" (meaning "life") and "gai" (meaning "value" or "worth"). It can be loosely translated as "a reason for being" or "a reason to wake up in the morning." Given we spend 80,000 hours[3] at work, wanting to wake up for them seems like an excellent starting place! And if that sounds like a lot of hours, Oliver Burkeman's book *Four Thousand Weeks*[4] embraces the finitude of life and extols us to reframe towards creating a meaningful life. I'm trying to instil some urgency here because I've seen what happens to postdocs who have been sat in the shadow for too long.

Ikigai represents the intersection of four fundamental elements: what you love, what you are good at, what the world needs and what you can be paid for. I have deliberately added in plurals for where the circles intersect. As the hugely talented researcher that you are, you could access multiple professions, passions, vocations and missions. This current set (you as an academic researcher into a specific topic) is a snapshot in the squiggly path of your career. You may create different foci for your ikigai as your career develops or hold a portfolio of roles in parallel that balance your ikigai.

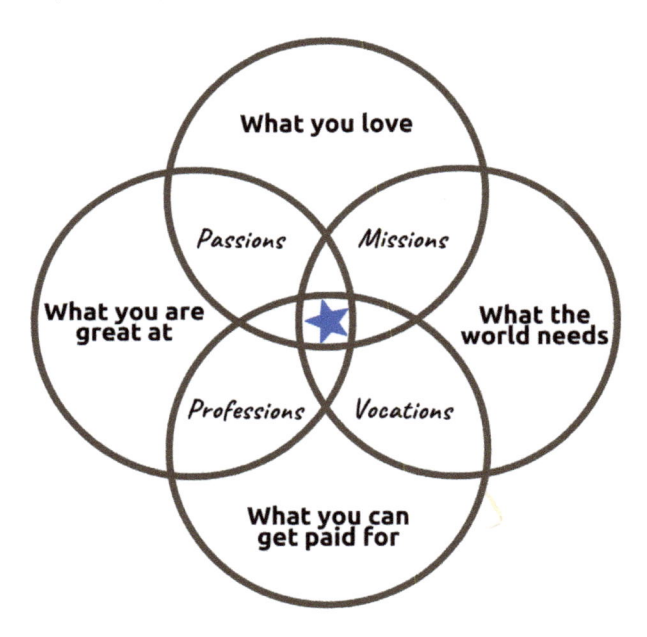

Ikigai Venn diagram showing four overlapping circles labeled "What you love", "What you are great at", "What the world needs", and "What you can get paid for", with intersections labeled Passions, Missions, Professions, and Vocations, and a star at the centre.

The following "light meter" questions based on ikigai not only help you take a snapshot of where you are but might well shine a light on what a future role should incorporate for you. I suggest you book out some peaceful time with yourself and record the answers. It is all too easy to skip over answers in our heads. Write, type or draw your thoughts as you explore the following. Focus on how you feel deep down (heart, gut, little toe – wherever you see your feelings inside you).

What you love Engaging in activities that bring you joy and satisfaction whilst pursuing your roles and interests. This is related to your passions (overlap with skills) and missions (overlap with what the world needs)

> Light meter question: What activities create feelings of enthusiasm and passion? Does your current role have these?

What you are great at Using your unique abilities, talents, and expertise (built from your experiences). It encompasses the things you are good at and the areas where you can excel. This is related to passions (overlap with what you love) and professions (overlap with what the world will pay you for)

> Light meter question: Which of your skills are true strengths (those that make you feel strong and energised)? Does your current role use these?

What the world needs Making a positive impact on the world, contributing to something larger than yourself, and meeting the needs of others, society or the planet. This is related to missions (overlap with what you love) and vocations (what the world will pay for).

> Light meter question: What issues fire you up with a desire to do something? Does your current role address these?

What the world will pay for Drawing a salary or creating an income stream from your activities. This is related to vocations (overlap with what the world needs) and professions (what you are great at).

> Light meter question: What level of income would support you living happily? Does your current role offer this?

This is big picture stuff (technical term!) but you are bright and sparky with skills and experiences flowing out of your eyeballs so why not create a career picture which maximises your ikigai? But I also know you like the facts and details and are time pressured. We can't take forever crafting our next step. The clock is ticking. Let us consider the elephant in the room … your contract.

Peak, Plateau or Plummet?

For me, one of the definitions of a postdoc is you are employed in a fixed-term contract working on a project someone else got the money for. This is usually your principal investigator (PI) who is most likely also your boss. There are a myriad of combinations and permutations in what constitutes a postdoc. The fact that no one seems to know how many postdocs there are in the UK I think highlights your special situation. My quest for numbers sent me on a circular mission of those agencies involved in higher education (HE)(even artificial intelligence (AI) gave up!). You are the engine house of academic research and yet neither a student (2.5 million of those in the UK) or academic staff (217,975 of those).[5] If postdocs are not counted, it would be tempting to think that you don't count. Harsh and very unfair. But perhaps this should spur you on to prioritise yourself a little more?

Fixed-term contract. Those dreaded words mean that for postdocs the clock is always ticking. Given getting a new role takes a minimum of four months (applying, interviewing, negotiating, notice periods), the clock is probably ticking louder than you thought. A prevailing view amongst postdocs is that you *should* stay to the end of your contract. For one contract to dovetail into another requires a chain of miracles (finding the perfect job at the perfect time for which you are the perfect candidate etc.). Wait until the end of your contract, and you will be looking for a job from the unenviable position of being unemployed. The first scenario is unrealistic and the second is a waste of your talent.

Shadows also get longer as the day draws on. The longer we stay in our postdoc roles the more pronounced those academic shadows get. Whether that is a long contract or a series, at some point you will need to move on. I am often asked how many postdocs is too many. To quote *Raiders of the Lost Ark*: "It's not the years, honey. It's the mileage." You could have had eight years of super productive, happy research fleshing out your CV or two years postdoc where the last year was at best treading water.

When should you move on from Planet Postdoc? Ideally you would move from one role to the next having reached the pinnacle of what that role can give you. Here I am talking about moving from being a postdoc to the next step (in academia or otherwise). It might be you build to peak postdoc through a series of postdoctoral positions. This might be the ideal launching point for a personal fellowship, academic tenure or exploring roles outside academia. But instead of leaving at "peak postdoc" people can wait too long and experience, at best, the "Postdoc Plateau". And trust me, the "Postdoc Plummet" is not the name of a fun theme park ride.

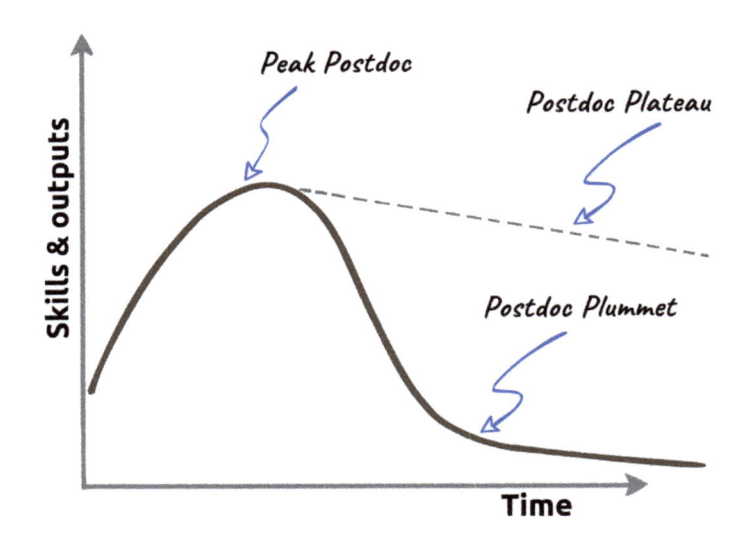

Peak Postdoc

That point where the postdoc role has given you all that it is going to give. Experiences, skills and your network have all been building to this point. The trajectory was upwards. The trouble with identifying this point precisely is that it is like trying to balance an egg – you are at a tipping point. You need to pay attention to your trajectory and check in with yourself regularly. It is better to leave on a high that might have got better than to fall into the next two categories.

Postdoc Plateau

Continuing in this, or the next postdoc, whilst keeping things ticking over. Publications may still happen but you are not adding anything new to your CV. More of the same is equivalent to a slow attrition in your worth to the next employer but more importantly to yourself. More of the same doesn't challenge or invigorate that mighty brain of yours. If you are not developing but everyone else in the marketplace is, then you are falling behind. The Plateau is a deceptively shallow slope. Postdocs in this situation report

- Doing research for research's sake
- Stuck in the same old rut
- I enjoy the bench work/library research (insert your day-to-day research graft here)

Postdoc Plummet

You have stayed too long. Your PI might not be able to deliver without you but you are no longer adding new skills; those around you are moving onto bigger and brighter things and the gap since the last "big" thing is growing. When I work with postdocs in this zone I often see

- Frustration (with yourself, others or the system)
- The feeling of being "just a postdoc" and not seeing how to move on
- A to-do list that is not focused on the metrics that point to academic success
- Anxiety, worry, sadness

It may be the case you now feel you *have to/should/could* move out from academic research but none of those sound enthusiastic! As an encouragement, I often get catch up emails along the lines of:

> *"Best move ever. Why didn't I do this sooner? I had not realised what it was going to be like. I found a home, got married (back to Jane Eyre)."*

It may be you are feeling you *should/could* consider the next academic step. What is stopping you moving on? Let's explore this more in the next chapter.

ENDNOTES

1. "Reader, I married him." *Jane Eyre* by Charlotte Brontë
2. British term for "a cup of tea" but feel free to expand the menu here.
3. 40 hours per week, 50 weeks per year, for 40 years according to the excellent career website https://80000hours.org/
4. https://www.oliverburkeman.com/books Oliver Burkman, *Four Thousand Weeks*, 2022, Vintage
5. https://www.hesa.ac.uk/news/19-01-2021/sb259-higher-education-staff-statistics Higher Education Statistics Agency (HESA), *Higher Education Staff Statistics: UK, 2019/20*, 2021

CHAPTER 2:
SHRUGGING OFF THE ACADEMIC COMFORT BLANKET

You are an intelligent person. Highly literate, highly numerate, a problem-solving, project-managing warrior. It is common to start beating ourselves up when we realise we have been sat in a dark place too long. Well stop that right now! Employ that big intellect on exploring the things that might have been keeping the lights off and hiding your path.

If we return to Sam's story, we had left them sitting in the dark having normalised many of academia's downsides. What had caused Sam to think about moving? Previously they had worked on a great project with an industry sponsor which had had extremely promising results. The project stalled and their levels of frustration rose. But they had glimpsed a world which might provide them with what they were missing:

- Clear deliverables and objectives set by management
- Good levels of accountability across the team supported by a good framework

- Challenges allowing personal growth presented within this scaffold

Creating these chinks of light and possibility for you is what this chapter is all about.

The itchy scratchy comfort blanket

It's okay. I understand how easy it is to get stuck. I like to think of academia as the itchy scratchy comfort blanket. It might have started as a beautiful robe – perhaps your graduation robe? We embraced the excitement of doing research and the feeling that this is where all these years of education have been leading. As time passes this robe settles like a blanket, quilting us in academia. As we grow and develop, we learn that not everything in academia is great: fixed-term contracts, the ever-turning hamster wheel of funding and the constant pressure to publish. The blanket gets dirty, itchy and has some prickly patches. And yet we know the rules of engagement, understand the career structures and are on our own territory. Our comfort zone.

My first experience of a weighted blanket comes to mind. These blankets full of little heavy beads are supposed to relax and comfort. It was reassuring but then I found I couldn't turn over easily. The blanket was heavy. Certainly, getting my arm out to switch on the light was tricky! Those wide-eyed moments of donning the academic gown got us here but in order to move on we are going to have to shrug off the comfort blanket and come blinking into the light.

Having coached postdocs for over twenty years, I know the blanket is woven from many threads including these really weighty ones:

- fears of the unknown – "What else could I do?"; "I don't know if I have the skills"
- sunk cost – "I've spent all this time getting to this point"
- asking the wrong people – "My PI says industry won't suit me"
- vocation – "I have always wanted to be an historian"; "I am a biochemist"
- there is no coming back – "Once you leave, you can't return"

The quotes are typical of those postdocs I work with. Note these are the weighty threads associated with negative feelings. There are postdocs who are excited about leaving or at least take a pragmatic approach that the outside world will be better balanced for them. In fact, the pragmatic leaver is currently coming out top in my online quiz (39% of postdoc respondents) with excited (27%) and cautious (23%) leavers following on. The quiz is based on responses by postdocs attending a career development event. This data is from the postdocs I work with and I am curious to see if readers of this book are different. If you would like to take the test then hop to https://www.riddle.com/view/Bpx3ajE6

The twilight zone (fears of the unknown)

"So this is my wish, a wish for me as much as it is a wish for you: in the world to come, let us be brave – let us walk into the dark without fear, and step into the unknown with smiles on our faces, even if we're faking them." – Neil Gaiman[1]

For a bunch of people whose job it is to push back the frontiers of knowledge, I sometimes doubt my own sanity when I hear this weighty thread from postdocs! Here our comfort blanket is protecting us from the monsters under the bed. Okay, some might be real or realisable but sitting imagining the worst is never helpful.

I see fear of the unknown as a major weighty thread in three types of postdoc leavers. The cautious, the uncertain and the autonomous.

Cautious would-be leavers embrace the unknown with a series of questions focusing on themselves. "Will I be good enough?", "Will I have the skills?", "Will I like the coffee?" (the last one is my business rider). There is a tendency to dwell and overanalyse the unknown without ever diving into uncovering the reality. Do enough of this and you will paralyse yourself. It is a sadly common downward spiral. The cause is fear of the unknown mixed with self-doubt. Undertake a realistic mapping of your skills, values and desires against your possible career options. This is where getting help from others, who can see your worth, can add a great deal of value.

Uncertain leavers embrace the unknown with a focus on the external. "What will it be like?", "What do they do?", "What are the differences from academic research?" This to me is the no-brainer section of the twilight zone as the answers are usually practical and easily discoverable. The key here is that questions focusing on the external (out of academia) usually can only be answered by going externally. As *The X-Files* had it: "The Truth is out there". I'll talk more about asking the right people later.

Autonomous would-be leavers question whether other roles could provide them with the same level of autonomy going forward. "Will I be able to choose my own direction?"; "Will I have control over my time?" Academia can provide a great flexible working environment too but it is very PI dependant. So those freedom seekers amongst us need to drill down into the true levels of autonomy that your next step, academic or otherwise, really offers. All roles come with constraints. In academia, these are largely set by the funders and their agendas, and by the academic hierarchy. The itchy bits of blanket. But have you investigated the levels of autonomy in choices outside? We may be assuming *all* industry roles are constrained by commercial realities. Find out so you are operating from fact not fiction.

> Unravel that thread
>
> *Identify your biggest unknown. The one that always leaps to mind when thinking of leaving. Write it down (important to articulate this). Underneath write down three concrete actions you can take to chip away at the unknown. Now take them!*

That sinking feeling (sunk cost fallacy)

"I've studied all this time." "I've racked up student loans." "This work could be turned into three papers." I hear these phrases from early career researchers time and time again. Often spoken by people who start the sentence with "I think I should move on but..."

These intellectual, financial and personal investments are the heavy threads of the comfort blanket. These are all an example of a sunk cost, a concept Nobel winning behavioural economist Richard Thaler[2] introduced the world. We commit the sunk cost fallacy when we continue a behaviour or endeavour because of previously invested resources (time, money or effort), even if (and this is the odd part) it would be beneficial to stop or switch. Not a rational decision but as humans we want to avoid those negative feelings associated with a loss. Our emotions make the decision.

Choosing to step away from an academic career opens us up to daunting negative feelings of loss. We arrive at any career crossroads with a back story full of hard-won victories and years of study. But to quote the first rule of holes, "If you are in a hole, stop digging". We need to turn "I've wasted all this time" (cost) into "I've invested in myself" (benefit). What do our experiences allow us to do *now*? What is our best return on that investment?

The work of David Ronayne, Daniel Sgroi and Anthony Tuckwell from the University of Warwick in 2021[3] identifies the factors of effort, belief, emotion and time alongside money as key drivers in being susceptible to the sunk cost fallacy. A research career is perhaps the perfect storm of all of these. We can create a tragic back story to rival the most tortured superhero. Reassuringly, they also highlight that the brain power required to avoid the fallacy is "slight" once we have noticed it.

This turns tragedy into trajectory.

Where does it manifest itself in the day-to-day life of researchers? A common scenario is still fretting about those papers you are a middle author on from six years ago that sit at the bottom of your former PI's to-do pile.[4] A huge amount of effort, worry and emotion is expended when quite often the postdocs concerned would be better off focusing on publishing current work. Our six years of fretting is holding us back from the clarity of understanding if the papers aren't written by now, they probably never will be.

The key here is to notice the language we use. We *know* we should move. This implies we have facts, information and experiences to bring to the decision. We *feel* we cannot. This implies our emotions may be having a disproportionate say in the matter. We need to engage our rational researcher brain.

> *Unravel that thread*
>
> *Create a simple list of positives/negatives for three non-academic realistic career options. If there are gaps in the facts, find out information from all sources – both factual (job descriptions) and personal (informational interviews, chats with connections in that industry). Interestingly when people dive into the information they score different job options using the same metrics that were holding them back through the sunk cost fallacy: salary (money), work/life balance (time and effort), happiness/fulfilment (emotion) and alignment with their values (belief). I have a sample score sheet for you in the Leaving Academia Toolkit (in the online resources)*

The anti-Terminator clause (I can't come back)

"I'll be back" is perhaps Arnold Schwarzenegger's most famous line.[5] The weighty thread of making a decision to leave academia and wanting to know if you can come back if it doesn't work out. I get completely the need for a safety net and postdocs who fall into this evaluator mode are often asking sensible questions. But no one can see the future perfectly. The lack of 100% surety can act as a paralysing agent. All career decisions involve, well, making one and leaping into a new role! You will have leapt several times before. There were probably lots of things you didn't know about your current role but you were never going to return to being a PhD student.

In their brilliant book *The Squiggly Career* Helen Tupper and Sarah Ellis highlight that modern careers are not the linear do-one-thing-your-whole-life affairs they were for my parents' generation. Our portfolio careers will be composed of different roles either serially or in parallel. Flexible working practices in terms of both time and location are increasingly prevalent since the Covid-19 pandemic. Careers that are a combination of academic research with industrial or professional practice, working in a start-up or spin-out or developing a consultancy alongside are all possibilities. It might well be possible to start something new *without* leaving. A couple of caveats are needed at this point.

- If you are just putting off the inevitable, then why not leap wholeheartedly now?
- Do not create a portfolio that has you operating at greater than 100% full-time work equivalent (different to your waking hours!). The number of brainy people I know who do this is astounding. Just because you *can* doesn't mean you *should*.

If you establish you can return, great. But will you want to? In my experience people who have moved out of academia discover careers they enjoy and aspects of themselves that perhaps had not had room to flourish before. This is supported by *Nature*'s postdoctoral survey[6] where postdocs are happier and better paid having made the move. At the very least embarking on a different role changes perspectives and develops our understanding of ourselves.[7]

Postdoc B has charted a career that has straddled university, industry and research institutes. Following two postdocs, they moved to a national laboratory followed by a further postdoc overseas. After that followed time working as a researcher in a large multinational company. A Daphne Jackson Fellowship[15] helped them to return to university scientific research. We join their story:

"I explored opportunities like an EPSRC mid-career fellowship and short-term postdocs, but just as I was adjusting to having an independent project funded the pandemic hit, causing financial constraints. I moved to a relatively new start-up company which wanted my technical skills.

I learnt lot in the multidisciplinary company and enjoyed many aspects of it. At the company decisions were made swiftly, perhaps even too swiftly for my taste. While some companies excel at quick decision-making, I felt this company wasn't receptive to the technical input. This sense of stagnation left me feeling there was no way forward. I valued rigour and aligned working styles and values with my ideal work environment.

My transition to a major research institute was driven by a desire to focus on research and working somewhere that appreciated technical competencies highly. I relished the technical aspects of my previous roles and found institute's work-life balance

> appealing. Being a staff scientist there allowed me to maintain my technical expertise. Having previously worked at a national laboratory, which had a commercial side, this move felt like a natural continuation. I am now involved in various projects, including image analysis and setting up pipelines."

There are researchers who have navigated the "there and back again route". Our postdoc story (see box) highlights one case where a fellowship dedicated to encouraging people to return was deployed. In a *Nature* article by Christine Ro four researchers detail their experiences of their time in industry "as a career-enhancing sabbatical".[8] What is clear is that as we grow in experiences our viewpoints will evolve. As marine ecologist Mariana Mayer-Pinto explains in the article:

"Sometimes you see polarization, such as that industry is better or academia is better. I feel we need to stop that. We should be complementary; rather than one being better or worse, it depends on what you want at a particular time of your life and what your interests are."

Unravel that thread

Imagine you had left academia and were looking to return. What would need to change for you to be happy?

I am who I am (vocation)

I wanted to be a scientist from around the age of four. I am not sure where the desire came from but it stuck. It carried me through my school years and into university. I was curious and driven to find out how things worked. How long have you been on your vocational academic track? Five years? Ten? If we include schooling that easily doubles. I do not use the term vocation lightly. I work with many researchers driven passionately to explore and learn their subjects.

A vocation encompasses those five sunk cost metrics of time, money, effort, emotion and belief perfectly.

No wonder that people explore the "just one more postdoc" route.

When it comes to leaving, this weighty thread of vocation manifests itself in two major ways aside from the sunk costs. Are you an expert or an enquirer? Obviously, you are both as a postdoc! I'm using these labels in the context of the weighty threads in our own particular itchy, scratchy comfort blanket.

The expert is secure in their knowledge. Being a subject matter expert defines them and is a crucial part of their identity. You enjoy your topic and know it inside out. There are roles "out there" that need experts. I have worked with postdocs who, somewhat to their surprise, have found roles in industry very much aligned to their discipline expertise. But don't expect these roles to have the perfect label for you. Academic expert jargon might differ from industrial labels despite, when it boils down to it, being the same subject. Experts will need to dig deep into roles to uncover the truth. Often, they have the required skillset in spades! I occasionally find myself wondering am I *still* a physicist? At one point it was a huge part of my identity and now it is part of my not so tragic backstory.

I do, however, know I use the scientific training my physicist identity gave me every day. The enquirer is focused on how the skills they have spent years building up will be deployed. They are also concerned how much and in what way a future role will stretch their cognitive powers. They are more process rather than subject matter focused compared to the expert. They need to know the how of a new role, including intellectual fit, rather than the what. Talking to people will be essential to finding a good future fit for the enquirer.

Unravel that thread

Is how you describe yourself a simple label (what you are) or a true descriptor (who you really are)?

Your PI doesn't have the answer (asking the wrong people)

Asking the wrong people. This reminds me of the joke with the two younger fish swimming along and an older fish passes them by with the greeting "Morning! How's the water?" The fish nod in reply and swim on. A little later one turns to the other and says "What on earth is water?" We can be blissfully unaware we are operating in a very specific environment. Elsewhere it is not normal to be surrounded by PhD types and not everything is measured with a H index.[9]

Academics are experts in their own field. They have got to where they are by being excellent at research and attracting money and influence to do more of the same. Academics are also well known for having opinions on everything. Challenging and understanding stuff is their role. But an academic is swimming in their own academic goldfish bowl. If they have spent their whole working life in and around universities, they aren't going to know anything about the wider world. After all the outside world thinks people at universities all have the summer off and wear lab coats all the time.

It seems natural to ask the people around you. But this is how myths about the outside world build up.

- "Oh, Rowan left the lab and was miserable." (No one has heard recently from Rowan).
- "There is no freedom in [insert role of your choice]." (Largely unfounded supposition).

You need to ask the people who can give you advice from their lived experience. And please do me a small favour? If you do move out, come back and let people know it is possible!

Also, if you are a brilliant postdoc (I'm sure you are) then your PI won't want you to leave. Why would they help and advise you to do something that is going to set back their agenda? And this is the important point about asking for advice or feedback. It is always coloured by that person's opinions and experiences. Tara Mohr, author of "*Playing Big*",[10] says:

> *The feedback doesn't tell you any facts about you; it tells you something about the perspective of the person giving the feedback*

This tells us we also need to talk to several people. You wouldn't rely on just one data point in your research, would you? And this doesn't have to involve a large networking blitz. You are probably already connected to research collaborators, old colleagues and friends from your degrees who are navigating other careers outside academia. I have found most people are perfectly willing to have a quick fifteen-minute video call about their careers. You need to turn on your career explorer mode.

Unravel that thread

Find three people like you who have left academia (use LinkedIn or similar to find them). Use an informational interview[11] with each to find out how and why they moved.

Sam overcame the itchy, scratchy comfort blanket. Shedding light on their situation helped them step out into a brighter world. On moving, they uncovered what they described as "realistic science". There were structures and processes (which often postdocs think might stifle) but these supported people who were enthusiastic, excited and attached to their projects. They found themselves working on tangible projects – once they were over the shock of ending the working day at 5.30 p.m. and having a lunch break! They were also constantly learning and developing which then opened possibilities for their next roles.

Are you ready to leave? The following sections will explore the factors in making the transition successful and what to do once you are there.

ENDNOTES

1. Neil Gaiman, *My New Year's Wish...*, December 31st, 2012, https://journal.neilgaiman.com/2012/12/my-new-years-wish.html
2. Thaler, R. 1980 *Toward a positive theory of consumer choice*. Journal of Economic Behavior & Organization, 1, 39–60
3. https://doi.org/10.1016/j.jebo.2021.03.029 Evaluating the sunk cost fallacy, *Journal of Economic Behaviour and Organization* 2021
4. Lawyers call these "smelly fish".
5. Said by him in eight movies not just The Terminator ones.
6. Chris Woolston *Nature* 587, 505-508 (2020) doi: https://doi.org/10.1038/d41586-020-03191-7
7. https://daphnejackson.org/about-fellowships/

8. Boomerang academics: why we left academia for industry, but then came back *Nature* 621, S99-S101 (2023) doi: https://doi.org/10.1038/d41586-023-03000-x
9. https://theconversation.com/explainer-what-is-an-h-index-and-how-is-it-calculated-41162
10. https://www.taramohr.com/tools-and-inspiration-for-playing-bigger/navigating-feedback/ Tara Mohr, *Playing Big: Practical Wisdom for Women Who Want to Speak Up, Create, and Lead,* 2015 Avery
11. A technical job-hunting term which boils down to a chat with someone 'in the know'.

SECTION TWO

UNRAVEL THE BLANKET AND BUILD A NET: GETTING READY TO MOVE ON

Leap, and the net will appear. – John Burroughs

Only in the leap from the lion's head will he prove his worth. – Indiana Jones and the Last Crusade

Decided to move on? Already heading to Monster? Sending off CVs into the ether?[1] Well take those twitchy fingers off the keyboard and wrap them around a mug instead! We have some work to do first. If you head off now, I can pretty much guarantee that you will be looking for a "non-academic" version of your existing role. I have witnessed that too many times. Now, it might be that is the perfect role for you but consider the wider picture a moment:

- If you are looking to move on from your role, at least one thing isn't perfect
- You are not the same person you were when you started on the academic path
- Other people can save you time, effort and heartache on this journey

- Autopilot career decisions are the worst. Take it from one who has been there and cried on the t-shirt
- Some threads from your academic blanket are precious, and some will bring you out in a rash

Every career move is a leap. You will never be 100% sure that it is going to work out. I can't sugar-coat that for you. So to make this next career move as proactive and positive as possible (try saying that fast) you need to weave three magic ingredients that will provide a tightrope, a safety/scramble net and a grappling hook. All much better than leaping into thin air like Indiana Jones in the quote above.

Your tightrope will be made up of some strong threads that are rooted in who you are and the path you want to tread. The next chapter will explore three essentials that can get overlooked in the rush to move on. You are absolutely worth taking some time to understand yourself. No one else can build that ikigai for you.

Ask any senior person "What has helped the most in your career?" and their network will be one of the top answers. We all need to curate our networks. I use the plural as we are often the link between different "nets" of people in our lives. Work, home, sports, hobbies. Networks provide advice, information and lived experience which give us a great sense of security (a safety net) that we are making the right moves (or avoiding the wrong ones). They can also sometimes help us "up the ladder" by referring us. But I think a scramble net might be a better metaphor. We can climb but we can also get tangled up (just me?). We need the right people to help us.[2]

Then we need to hook the right role. We need to create compelling evidence of our skills, experiences and potential that can be launched firmly in the direction of our new would-be employers. A grappling hook might sound dramatic[3] but we will find out it is a job to get a job.

You have realised a move out of academia is on the cards but ask yourself if you are stopping yourself in any of the following ways:

- I just need to get a certificate for this ... (what you have to offer)
- I just need to talk to one more person ... (who you need to talk to)
- I will apply a little later on in my contract ... (what you need to be able move on)

The next three chapters explore each of these barriers and boost you beyond them to be able to apply to your next role. Chapter 3 will be focusing on you and pulling out those threads that make you unique and valuable to the wider world. Chapter 4 is all about the other people in our lives who will influence our career journeys in a variety of ways. And chapter 5 gets you focused on some key aspects of your job acquiring toolkit.

Don't forget your friendly Leaving Academia Toolkit will provide a practical framework once you have explored your tightrope, net and grappling hook. Head to the online resources to access it.

ENDNOTES

1. From Greek mythology: the upper regions of the atmosphere; clear sky or heaven
2. https://www.linkedin.com/pulse/new-survey-reveals-85-all-jobs-filled-via-networking-lou-adler/
3. It always makes me think of Batman zooming up a building.

CHAPTER 3: PULL YOURSELF TOGETHER: THREADS OF GOLD, STEEL AND PURPLE

> *"Oh, for God's sake, pull yourself together, man. You're going into the forest, after all."* – Argus Filch, Harry Potter and the Philosopher's Stone[1]

> *"No man ever steps in the same river twice, for it's not the same river and he's not the same man."* – Heraclitus[2]

We are all wonderfully evolving beings, and the world is rapidly evolving too. At every transition we need to take stock of who we are and where we stand, now. We need to pull together a renewed picture of who we are, tugging on the threads that serve us and discarding those that don't.

With the twenty-twenty vision of hindsight, I can now see the evolution in my career as slowly understanding and picking up those threads that really matter to me. My PhD emphasised my love of practical creativity, my postdoc years highlighted the skills I enjoyed, my time in professional services demonstrated I needed to see the impact of my work and being a business owner calls me to be brave and resilient every single day. These are my tightrope threads – it's quite a thick rope now. There are plenty of threads that I've left behind at each transition. We unravel and then we weave. The trick is to pick the right threads.

The golden thread (your values)

Gold. Silver. Platinum. All have been used for centuries to make beautiful objects. The golden thread here is not directly visible but possibly even more precious. Your values.

> *Your values are the things that you believe are important in the way you live and work. They (should) determine your priorities, and, deep down, they're probably the measures you use to tell if your life is turning out the way you want it to.*[3]

Our values are tied to our internal beliefs. The outside world sees our values through our attitudes and behaviours. I think this is why I have always struggled to pin them down because by their very nature they aren't tangible and yet once we identify them there is a feeling of certainty. Of rightness.

And this is why our next career step requires us to look within and identify what is important to us now. We will be building decisions on a concrete base. Values are internal and time bound. We need to identify *our* values, not those imposed by academia or family. And although some may stay with us for life, others may surface as we and our circumstances change. I value, and therefore make time for, my parents as we all get older. My teenage self would never have done that!

Once we understand our values it becomes easier to navigate the wealth of possible career choices the average postdoc faces. You *could* do almost anything; our values provide us with a steer on the *should*. A personal, heartfelt set of reasons that will help define if the next leap in our squiggly career feels the right one.

I know you want to get going but understanding your values is really going to make things easier in the long run. Block out some "me" time and do some mental heavy lifting. There are several ways to tap into our values and I've highlighted some resources at www.thenerdcoach.co.uk/leaving_academia. My favourite method I have nicknamed "good day, bad day".

Think to the last time you experienced a great moment. Things felt in flow, you were happy/content/proud of what you had done. Hold that feeling whilst you jot down as a paragraph or single words the following:

- What specifically had you been doing?
- Why were you feeling so great?
- Who, if anyone, were you with?
- What other factors, if any, were involved?

Repeat it for other peak times and great moments. These positive experiences are key elements to identify as we build future careers.

Built up a bank of happy memories? Good. Keep them safe because sometimes it can be easier to identify our values when someone or something stomps on them. The bad day scenario is where you felt frustration, anger and/or a sense of loss. Ask the questions above replacing "great" with "dreadful".

Use that researcher brain of yours to untangle the commonalities from the stories. Develop those themes into a list of ten or so values. Values don't just have to be one word. Can you now rank your list? It might be helpful to take them a pair at a time and decide which one is an absolute must-have. If you want a starting list of values, I find James Clear's[4] a great starting place.

Weave a thread

What would your next step look like if you were solely focused on your golden thread? Where would your values fit best?

The steel thread (your strengths)

Apparently, spider silk is stronger than steel[5] but as a lifetime arachnophobe[6] we will go for steel as the emblem of tough and strong. Your strengths are the steel thread.

One of the reasons I love working with researchers on their careers is the sheer wealth of possibilities that your skill set gives you. It is worth repeating: you are highly literate, numerate, problem-solving, project-managing warriors.

Chapter 3: Pull yourself together: threads of gold, steel and purple

A simple list of the things you tackle (on top of the actual research) in one day will highlight this:

- Booker Prize levels of creative writing (describe your research project in this 100-word abstract)
- UN levels of negotiation (agreeing an author list)
- Olympic levels of endurance (University committee meetings)
- Oprah levels of empathy (consoling the master's student, again)
- Mad Men marketing skills (departmental open day)

You have spent years honing your research skills (discipline knowledge and techniques). As researchers, you will be *good*[7] at many things. But if we are to enjoy our next role, we need to be doing slightly more than those things which we are simply good at. I prefer this definition of a strength:

> *"A strength is an activity that helps you, makes you feel strong. It's something that when you're doing it, you're energized, you can feel passionate about it. You really want to do it. The opposite of that, a weakness, is something that just ... drains the life out of us."*[8]

How would you answer the overly used interview question "What are your strengths?" using the definition above. Seriously, imagine yourself in that interview answering honestly what makes you feel really energised and fired up. What things would you do happily and suddenly discover hours had passed? Once you have the answer to that question, you know that any fun future role needs to include plenty of it!

You need to step away from any threads of the academic blanket that got there through our training, experiences and discipline knowledge that just don't, at the risk of sounding like Marie Kondo, bring you joy. When moving on from my postdoc, my most marketable skill was my ability to programme (seven years' experience of supercomputing) but there is simply not enough coffee and chocolate in the world to have made me energised enough to be a programmer professionally. My strengths are creativity, being able to pull together disparate information to solve problems and working visually. Certainly, my undergraduate degree didn't play to these strengths, but I have been stepping more and more into them. Don't be tempted to describe yourself with what you think makes a good biologist/historian/engineer.

Identifying your strengths is perhaps easier than looking at your values. For one thing we can ask others for their views. When I have done this, there have always been pleasant surprises. Strengths I had not seen in myself but on reflection make sense. There are various methods to do this outlined in the online resources. When you ask people make sure you ask for specific examples to help you put their comments in context.

Preferences, both personal and professional, are aligned to our strengths. Whilst you are in "taking stock" mode it could be helpful to undertake a personality assessment. But please avoid random quizzes on the internet! Three I have personally found helpful are MBTI,[9] Strengths Finder[10] and Belbin Team Roles.[11] They do all have a cost associated with them but check with your institution as to what they offer. I have yet to meet a researcher who wants to be "put into a box" but these assessments give us information to wrestle with and a structured way to reflect.

> *Weave a thread*
>
> *What would your next step look like if you were solely focused on your steel thread? Where would your strengths be used most?*

The purple thread (your courage)

"Courage calls to courage everywhere, and its voice cannot be denied" – Millicent Fawcett

The final strand in our personal threads takes its colour from the suffragette movement in the early 1900s. Their colours (adopted as my brand colours) were white for purity, green for hope and purple for dignity. This is perhaps the most important thread as it calls us to courageously respect and honour ourselves. To hold our heads up high as we approach the next step in our careers. The world doesn't owe you a living (an entitled stance) but it is okay to portray and promote your best self to the world. It is okay to pursue for you.

Changing roles is scary and changing sector (as we move out of academia) is perhaps doubly so. A friend described it as wailing at a new coal face, convinced we don't have the knowledge and skills to tackle it. And yet what the world is asking postdocs to bring to the table is seldom solely knowledge based. You have spent a lifetime learning *how* to tackle problems. I could ask you "How would you go about creating robot rabbits?" and even though this isn't your field (if it is I want to know!) you will have already had three thoughts about where and how to look for information. This is not something everyone can do! And this is just one of the many amazing things about you.

We need to gather the gold and steel threads and look for roles that can bring us personal joy and challenge. You are amazingly qualified (having a PhD is *not* normal), experienced (yes, your PhD counts as time served!) with a toolkit of transferrable skills that are highly desirable so why on earth do so many of you feel rooted to the spot like a rabbit in the headlights? I think there are two big aspects that mean we have lost sight of our purple thread here.

Many of the postdocs I work with have a great sense of duty. This is towards your group, your boss, your project or the discipline. I don't think it is too grand to say you are committed to "The Work" (capitals intended). If we come back to Sam's story: no one had ever left the lab, the project was important for people's health, and they felt indebted to academia. Your sense of duty and the research setting are a perfect recipe for reluctance and guilty feelings at the thought of moving on. There is also possibly the (unhealthy, irrational) survivors' guilt of getting this far in academia.

> *Guilt is the emotion we feel if we let ourselves or others down by failing to meet a particular standard.*[12]

But you do need to ask the more important question here. What do I owe to myself? You are a bright, articulate person who could serve the world in multiple ways; no one said you had to sacrifice yourself to do it. In fact, if you are happy and motivated then you will be doing much better at what you decide to do. Feelings of duty and guilt can be helpful in pointing us forward but only if they are based in rationality. But asking ourselves what we deserve can seem very unnatural! A starting point might be to write down all the things you would wish for and recommend to a friend in your situation (chances are you know a few!).

Academia is at its best a meritocracy and at its worst a pit of vipers. A grown-up version of the children's game snakes and ladders. The quest for knowledge and the pushing back of frontiers has created a hierarchal system with super demanding and, at times, conflicting metrics (postdocs must publish, publish, publish but to apply for a lectureship position you need to have a teaching track record). You are surrounded by people with accolades[13] all in the search of the next big thing. Academia's very nature encourages us to compare. Too often you are measuring what you are not (yet) rather than what you have got.

Revisiting Sam's story they felt they were becoming a perfectionist. Striving to make their work better and better had crystalised a belief that they couldn't do "stuff". This type of thinking is where I see the word "only" (and its sneaky friend "just") creep in. These doubts and fears whilst natural are not helpful, and viewed from outside academia are not actually true. Can you turn around the following statements?

"I am only a quantum biologist postdoc."

"I only have two years on this project."

"My PhD was in a different area to my postdoc."

"I only use programming to analyse my data; I'm not a computer scientist."

It is time to stop judging yourself against the Nobel Prize winners and honestly appraise yourself against some real-world job descriptions. Find one external job that interests you (your gold thread) that needs some of your beloved strengths (your steel thread). Choose anything at all, the further away from your current role the better. Drill down into the person specification and jot down any evidence at all for each point it mentions. No "onlys" or "justs" allowed. The first time you do this is difficult so co-opt a trusted friend to help if needed.

Weave a thread

What would your next step look like if you were solely focused on your purple thread? Are you courageously choosing a future for you?

Chapter 3: Pull yourself together: threads of gold, steel and purple 47

In order to take the next steps you need to have belief in yourself and give yourself permission to seek out a brilliant career.

Whilst each of these threads are important, it is in the combination that we have a strong career model. A single strand of rope can be tough but three strands combined are much stronger. Most rope will be three strands twisted under tension.[14] This is the rope you would find on tall sail ships and was so precious that it was often defined with a "rogue's thread" to deter theft. Goethe wrote in 1809[15]

> *Every rope in the English Navy has a red thread running through it, which cannot be extracted without unravelling the whole, so that even the smallest length of rope can be recognised as belonging to the crown.*

Your rope will be individual for you. Whether it is twisted or braided for even more strength, the smallest length of your career tightrope should be identifiably you. Every choice you make needs to be guided by it.

ENDNOTES

1. Or *Sorcerer's Stone* for non-Brits. JK Rowling *Harry Potter and the Philosopher's Stone* 1997 Bloomsbury Publishing PLC
2. He lived c. 6th century BCE and his quotations are attributed by later authors. His book is lost.
3. https://www.mindtools.com/a5eygum/what-are-your-values
4. James Clear wrote *Atomic Habits* (2018 Random House Business) and his website is very useful https://jamesclear.com/core-values
5. https://youtu.be/UGcOKR-Aojs?si=WTAM-qEHJ-WCMoJ2
6. Made so much worse by an fMRI study I conducted during my PhD.
7. Probably excellent as researchers are far too modest.
8. Marcus Buckingham, *Go Put Your Strengths To Work,* Simon & Schuster 2007
9. https://eu.themyersbriggs.com/en/tools/MBTI/MBTI-Step-I
10. https://www.gallup.com/cliftonstrengths/en/254033/strengthsfinder.aspx
11. https://www.belbin.com
12. https://www.mindtools.com/ajkye4s/dealing-with-guilt
13. a touch on a person's shoulders with a sword at the bestowing of a knighthood.
14. https://www.knotandrope.com/blogs/dressing-the-knot/3-strand-vs-braided-rope
15. Johann Wolfgang Goethe Die Wahlverwandtschaften 1809 (Elective Affinities)

CHAPTER 4:
DEALING WITH OTHERS: THE GOOD, THE BAD AND THE ...

Alex was a researcher looking to move from one laboratory to another one in a different institution where they would have responsibility for running a scientific service and research. Alex started our meeting by apologising: "Oh, I've decided not to apply as it's too big a leap". This shocked me because even though the field was not mine, Alex's CV and the job description could not have been a better match. An absolute no-brainer to apply. In fact, I had wondered if they were aiming high enough. Delving down into the reasons for the change in heart, every single member of their current lab had told them it was too big a leap. This putting people down and back into a box of someone else's design makes me furious. This is an extreme example but feedback is always coloured by other people's viewpoints. I asked Alex to take me through the job description line by line. Reader, Alex applied, was accepted and negotiated a pay increment over the baseline.

People are a key ingredient in moving forward in our careers. You need advice, insight, direction and references from them. Even Lego Batman ("I work alone") realised he needed others in the end. But as Alex's story shows us, people can help or hinder (and sometimes both!). You need to take a grown-up approach to your interactions to provide safety nets and rope ladders whilst avoiding getting snagged on a loop.

Asking for help

Alex had asked for advice and had received a big, negative consensus – from people who might well have suffered from their absence in the laboratory. It is very natural to seek the views of those in your immediate environment. You probably interact with them every day and chances are they share similar backgrounds and even roles. You might have friendly interactions or even be friends, but this does not qualify them to be the perfect people to ask for advice.

Let us start with you, oh wise one. Tara Mohr recommends that people tap into listening to their wise future-self having first visualised who this might be. She calls this your inner mentor.[1] Shirzad Chamine talks about us having an inner sage which can combat our personal saboteurs.[2] The key here is that we might well be a lot wiser than we think! Or feel. Listening to our sagely selves can be a great step. This comes back to your purple thread of courageous self-respect. Weigh up advice, think about suggestions but trust yourself first and foremost. The other people don't have to make the career leap. You do.

As someone moving on you will have a whole host of questions. When it comes to careers, I think there are three groups of others who can really add value. This is true of both academic and non-academic careers.

- People a little way on the journey or paths you are considering – think three to five years out. They will be able to speak to current practices and still remember leaping vividly.
- People outside the journey with no vested interest. They will be your sounding boards, cheerleaders and constructive challengers. These might be friends, family, careers professional or coach.[3]
- People who have been in the paths you are considering for a while (five years plus). They will be able to give a larger context from their experience and put you in touch with more of the first group. Sam had identified someone in this group who was really pivotal in helping them make the transition from academia.

Use those phenomenal research skills of yours to find them. Hit your search engine of choice or even better start using LinkedIn effectively.[4] Once you have found them you need to politely approach them and ask for help. I know you are a super self-reliant researcher but it is okay to ask for help and advice.

If you don't ask you already have your no. If you do ask, chances are you will have your know.

If you are polite and specific, the very worst that can happen is someone saying no (more likely you just won't get a reply). It is my experience that 90% of people will reply positively to a request where they know exactly what the other person wants. So, there are three rules for requests:

1. Keep it brief and to the point. They need to know who you are but not your life history.
2. Let them know specifically what you are looking for. "I'd like to know about what day-to-day life as a rabbit roboteer looks like."
3. Protect and respect their time. "It would be great to have a 15-minute video call with you."

Ah, I forgot rule #0 – never, ever ask for a job! These chats are for help and advice, not for begging and pleading. Adam Grant divides people into three types when it comes to asking for a favour: takers, matchers and givers.[5] In asking for help you can always pay it back in some way or pay it forward (help someone else). A lovely way to finish up might be to ask if there is anything you could do for them. In fact, there is a call to action at the end of this book to do just that! Always say thank you and send a note afterwards. There is nothing better than a note in your inbox saying you helped someone.

A note on how to hold an informational interview. The key is to become an expert listener. The people you will be talking to are in the know. Give them a platform to share their wisdom with you. If you go in with a barrage of questions you may well miss some key information.

Better to use the RASA framework developed by Julian Treasure:[6]

- **Receive** Give them your full attention (a beautiful gift) by looking at them and facing them.
- **Appreciate** Nudge the conversation along with little noises, nodding and body language.
- **Summarise** Everyone's time is precious. Use "so" to summarise a point (and check understanding) and move onto your next topic of questions.
- **Ask** questions and check in your understanding as you go along. Try to use open questions which encourage lists of possibilities. "Who else would be great to talk to?" rather than "Can you recommend someone to talk to?"

Collate your evidence (you didn't just ask one person, did you?) and weigh up what that means for you going forward. Is the information in concert with your values (golden thread)? Are the skills they need part of your steel thread? Does it sound courageous, exciting and enticing (purple thread)? It is perfectly fine if the answer is no! As a researcher you have a wealth of career doors open to you at this point. If you close (or slam) some doors shut then you are closer to finding out the ideal career routes.

Curating your network

I know this section title sounds a little Machiavellian[7] but networks do not spring into life overnight and need a certain amount of nurturing to keep them ticking over. If you have a goal in mind then certainly some of your existing network can help you (if they know about it) but you will also need new connections. In writing this book (my third), I have actively sought out experts and champions as well as tapping into my existing network. My experience has been less lonely, better informed and a great deal more fun this time around.

In their book "*Who is in your personal boardroom?*" Zella King and Amanda Scott[8] talk about forming a boardroom of twelve people covering twelve roles for those who have a specific goal in mind. For those who are setting out on a career goal the following roles are particularly important:

- **Navigators** are familiar with the context, politics and personalities in the sector you are considering. An industry insider for example.
- **Challengers** will sense check your thinking and with any luck point out the (what should be) obvious. These could be trusted friends, mentors or coaches. My greatest challenger brings out the best in me with her insightful questions.
- **Unlockers** access resources: time, money, people. They might get you time with an expert or find some funding for training. Researcher development offices are great unlockers!
- **Influencers** work behind the scenes for you. They might have a word with the next person you need to talk to, write you a reference or publicise your work. In my world these are my clients who refer me to others.

Now I don't think you need to be as structured as the 12/12 model but you do need to curate into your network people who can help you move on. This is not collecting names on LinkedIn – next to useless if that is all you do. You are looking for quality over quantity. You have to inform and engage with people. If we were selling a product we might talk about building "know, like and trust".

- **Know** – how and what do people know about you? We talk about online presence in the next section but what is people's first contact with you like? For existing contacts, do they know what direction you are now interested in?
- **Like** – what would attract people into your network? Similar skills, experiences, places, interests. Although we are looking to move on professionally, we need to remember we and our network are humans! Don't forget those you share sporting or social activities with are part of your network too. Enter into a dialogue with people (get chatting!).
- **Trust** – what would help convince people you were worth mentioning to others who might help you? This might involve helping them out in some way or demonstrating your knowledge or expertise. Be on the lookout to add value to your network: sending on an interesting article, putting two people together.

Curation isn't just about network growth. As you develop a network of people who can help you with the next step there will be less time available from you to those who aren't actively helping at this point. This might be part of the natural ebb and flow of friendships and connections.

But if there are people in your network who are actively stopping you from developing, exploring and reaching your full potential then you need to step away from them. Those who erode the boundaries set by our values, diminish our strengths to prevent us from growing into them, and cause us to lose faith and courage are actively unravelling our personal tightrope. Alex's laboratory was full of people who for various reasons were holding them back. Alex had moved on in more ways than one.

Researcher C has always possessed a strong sense of direction in her career decisions, achieving remarkable progress in just four years since graduation. Her journey began with a Canadian hospital safety role, where she quickly realised her passion for building and designing products. This prompted a shift towards research and development, focusing on human-centred design. Her ability to align her thesis project with an industry sponsor showcased her external-facing compass for career choices. She actively sought work experiences during her university years, completing three internships that catapulted her into senior roles upon graduation. We join her story:

"My career path led me to prominent automotive organisations, where I thrived in high-performing teams.

My approach involved applying for opportunities before I felt completely ready, understanding that my skills would catch up. Journaling my life aspirations for the next 10, 5, and 1 years proved a powerful practice for me. I realised that I didn't want to be confined to climbing the corporate ladder. I embarked on a journey of motherhood, followed by a career move. In 2019, I chose to take voluntary redundancy and joined another automotive company hoping for a possible sideways move into another sector. It turned out to be a brief but intense experience!

My resilience was tested as I navigated challenges, including 14 interviews and five offers before landing the job I'd been after. Despite initially finding what I was looking for, a toxic culture prompted me to seek new opportunities. A recruiter in the banking sector offered me a chance to build a research team. My knack for negotiation resulted in a 53% salary increase when I moved further across business units because I'd done my homework on the going rate and was determined not to be the cheap, internal candidate.

I encourage others to continuously interview for their next role, network, and remain open to opportunities even when they feel unprepared. It's about seizing chances and having faith that skills and abilities will develop along the way."

Difficult conversations

Once we have decided to move out of academia, we are going to have to tell other people. Your newly curated network will be providing people you can ask for help, advice and information.

I have always found there is a clarity in conversation – the act of saying something out loud to another human crystalises our thoughts. So, I would encourage you to have your initial conversations with trusted friends or mentors. These will fortify you as you pull the toolkit we discuss in the next section together.

You are right to be making a positive decision for you but there will be wider effects for other people. In conversations be mindful of this and think about how that person might best like the information, what questions they might have and what your decision might mean for them. In his excellent book *The Big Leap*, Gay Hendricks[9] explains that part of "the genius move" is to realise that there is no way in the universe that will allow us to control what other people think and feel about our decisions. That is up to them. Let that soak in for a moment. I for one have spent far too much of my time on this planet wondering, second guessing and frankly trying to see into the future especially when it comes to difficult conversations.

On reflection I have learnt two things. The first is that we need to be kind and considerate to ourselves as well as our counterpart. The second is we can over scare ourselves. I have worked with many postdocs who have been gearing up to dreaded conversations. They have created a mountain in front of them. And when I see them again it was not nearly as bad as they had feared. Much more molehill than mountain. This quote always comes to mind:

> *"I don't want to be in a battle. But waiting on the edge of one I can't escape is even worse."* – Pippin, The Return of The King, J.R.R. Tolkien

Explaining your decision to family and friends might be a good start. But don't be surprised if they echo some of the threads from the academic comfort blanket! I can still remember my mum asking me "Are you sure? You've spent all these years getting here!" despite supporting my decision. Given I was leaving to become a full-time mum for a while, I wasn't prepared for the wealth of (unsolicited) opinions on the subject! Remember that other people's feedback is always based on their viewpoint. It may well tell you much more about them than help you!

When you start telling the rest of the world (well your part of it) is up to you. Some people tell people as they are about to embark on searches and interviews and others wait until they have a job offer all sewn up. Largely for postdocs, this will boil down to how supportive your Principal Investigator is. Some are fantastic managers, and some are dreadful. But they all have the following things in common:

- They have worked hard to write many grants. Only a percentage of these will be successful (less than 20%). One of these funds your research

- The grant needs to deliver outcomes within the project time frame
- Great postdocs like you are becoming harder to recruit
- Recruiting is time-consuming and painful

Be mindful of this when announcing your decision and step into their shoes. Can you create an exit strategy that makes life as pain-free as possible for all concerned? Fold this pre thinking into your preparation.

You are holding more cards than you think. Legally you are perfectly entitled to give notice that you are moving on. Typically, this is around a month (check your contract). You do not have to stay to finish the project or write up papers. In fact, those might now be much less important to you career-wise. But the world is a small place and no one should burn bridges if they can possibly avoid it. You need to balance the desires of your future employer (start as soon as possible), your PI's (stay as long as possible) and yours (I'd like a gap of at least five minutes between roles).

For the conversation itself, have just that. Do not resign by email, ask for a private meeting in your PI's diary. Preferably away from the speculative eyes of the rest of the research team. Be prepared for this to be a short meeting as your PI might need to think through next steps. A few tips:

- Stick to the facts of the situation.
- It may be a fact you are unhappy where you are but don't ever accuse people or the system. Stick to "I" statements. I feel I need to move on.

- Be mindful you are choosing a career course your PI has not; try not to malign their career.
- It is okay to feel emotional but try to keep a level head. Don't try to match any emotions that come back towards you, especially anger.
- Ask politely what the next steps should be and when you should meet again.

Take yourself for a walk afterwards to clear your head. You've just taken an essential step forward to leaving academia.[10][11][12]

The net we weave

This chapter is not a tick box exercise. Our net(work) is a constantly evolving collection of threads, splices (forging connections) and knots (tricky bits). As we will see later Sam's network helped them evolve from peak to peak. This transition may be a major first but it will not be your last. And of all the connections ensure you have people with whom you can mutually cheer, champion, challenge and cherish:

> *"...the real purpose of a coven was to meet friends, even if they were friends simply because they were really the only people you could talk to freely as they had the same problems and would understand what you were moaning about."* – Wintersmith, Terry Pratchett

ENDNOTES

1. https://www.taramohr.com/book/inner-mentor-signup/
2. https://www.positiveintelligence.com/saboteurs
3. Choose wisely if dipping into friends or family. Objectivity isn't everyone's natural talent.
4. Honestly it's not that bad and I have a course to help you. See the www.thenerdcoach.co.uk/leaving_academia/ for your offer.
5. https://adamgrant.net/quizzes/give-and-take-quiz/
6. https://www.juliantreasure.com/5-part-video-series/rasa
7. Beautiful word for someone who operates an end justifies the means philosophy.
8. https://www.personalboardroom.com
9. Gay Hendricks *The Big Leap: Conquer Your Hidden Fear and Take Life to the Next Level* 2010 HarperOne
10. https://stemleaders.oregonstate.edu/leaving-research-group
11. https://www.linkedin.com/pulse/how-tell-your-advisor-youre-leaving-academia-doug-kalish/
12. https://www.judyringer.com/resources/articles/we-have-to-talk-a-stepbystep-checklist-for-difficult-conversations.php

CHAPTER 5: BUILDING YOUR TOOLKIT

Have you heard of the old adage "What got you here, won't get you there"?[1] You are entering the world beyond academia (you have shrugged off that blanket haven't you?[2]). That world needs your skills and experiences but ... and here's the rub ... on their terms. Only academics speak academic and thankfully most organisations aren't run like universities.

I know you are desperate to get going but entering the non-academic world with your current CV (you kept it current, yes?) is like taking a beautiful, hand engraved 18th century sword to a gun fight. It's going to be brief and messy. And it's not just the CV we need. You are going to have to build an appropriate toolkit that presents you in the best light that can snag that next position. It's time for the grappling hook.

It's a job to get a job

Most postdocs I work with can readily reel off a list of things they need to do to get a job. Trouble is they always go a little quiet when I ask the question: "*When* are you going to do this?"

A conservative estimate of moving from one role to another, if you saw the perfect job advertised today, is around four months. Closing date, shortlisting, interview schedule, decisions, notice periods ... all things beyond your control. And that is if you were perched on the starting blocks ready to tailor your application in the career equivalent of the 100m.

Being on the starting blocks means having done the big thinking this book has pointed at so far, discovered where and how to look for positions, leveraged the power of your network and then got all your external facing ducks in row (feedback on your CV, online presence, draft cover letter).

Archimedes apparently said, "Give me a lever long enough and a fulcrum on which to place it, and I shall move the world". If you want to move your world you need to invest a good amount of time in the preparation stage (the lever) and then pivot it in a perfect way for that particular job (fulcrum).

Okay I'll stop with the metaphors because hopefully it has hit home that you are going to need to invest a decent amount of time into your career at this point. And yes, I know it is already on top of the ever so relaxed (not) post-doc contract. But if you want something done, ask a busy person.

So how can we create time we don't have? This book is a case in point. I wrote this with a cohort of three other amazing women all of whom were running businesses or holding down high-powered jobs. But we prioritised the writing and then made time. Most of the words you've read (thank you) were written between six and seven a.m. over two months. There was coffee. But it resulted in incremental daily progress. The other unexpected effect it created was a constant, low-level focus on my project for the rest of the day.

I extoll you to spend a *reasonable* amount of *focused* time *every* day on your career. Just focus for a set amount of time on pushing your career goals further. Be specific in your tasks – don't just mindlessly scroll job pages. The daily practice will push your career up your agenda by raising awareness. It will hopefully become a lens through which you can notice opportunities and maximise attendance at events.

What is a reasonable amount of time? Take the amount of time left on your contract and subtract four months. This is the maximum time you have to get on the starting blocks. You do not have to stay to the end of your contract. If this time is either negative or you are truly inspired to move on quickly then I would recommend investing at least one hour a day in your next step. It is now your job to get a job.

Head to The Leaving Academia Toolkit to plan out your career campaign. I have checklists of five, fifteen and forty-five minute tasks that will move you forward with your job search.

Stop looking like a postdoc

If we are creating a grappling hook then the hook parts really need to capture the attention of a would-be employer.

Academia wants postdocs; the world wants big data programmers, policy advisors and project managers to name a few. Ways you might be looking like a postdoc:

- Your introductions start "I'm a postdoc at …"
- Research associate on LinkedIn
- Your LinkedIn About section describes your research project, not your skills
- A CV which starts with your academic credentials
- A CV which highlights universities worked at over roles performed
- A LaTeX formatted CV (although it can look great!)
- Citing bibliometrics
- Lists of conferences/meetings/students/papers
- Jargon dense external assets

Dress for the job you want is an old bit of advice, but here I want you to create all your external facing assets pivoted towards the job you want. This is much easier if you have narrowed down what you would like to do. If that is the case, you can start crafting a tailored CV and write your LinkedIn "About" as almost a cover letter to your ideal employer. Niching your approach really works well because the employer can immediately see your relevance to them. A broad-brush approach is just too difficult: in appealing to everyone, you appeal to no one. This is why generic CVs often bounce. When I hear the phrase "I've sent my CV off to lots of places and not heard back" it's usually because it was a *singular* CV.

You need to woo employers. Echoing the language they use, their terminology and highlighting the particular things about you that mean you will be an asset to them. We don't have to guess at this! As you build up your information from chats with your network, internet research and from reading job descriptions you will start to collect phrases, skills and experiences that are key to moving into those roles. This is where you start your pitch to the outside world.

Once armed with a clear picture of what employers are looking for the best way to un-postdoc your application is to ditch your old CV and rebuild in a new format. Typically, academics use a chronological (and sometimes chronic[3]) format. The order of the sections is what appeals to academia. By swapping to a skills-based CV format you instantly have to choose which skills to put first

If you want a beautifully tailored application, there is no better way than talking to the person in the advert mentioned as the "further information" contact. Email them and ask for a brief chat. Open your chat with a question such as: "How did this role come about?" The aim is to get them to spill the beans on what the role and organisation are like. Use the RASA framework from the previous chapter. Do not send your CV at the point of asking – you are going to tailor it!

Head to The Leaving Academia Toolkit to raise your game on presenting yourself to the world. Explore checklists for LinkedIn and advice on CVs that shine.

Salary is a lonely word

Too often the focus is solely salary when we are looking at the next position. I absolutely get why that might be a big factor (we all need food and shelter), but I want to encourage you to look at the whole picture.

You are bright and sparky (no arguing) and deserve a next step that challenges, excites and fulfils you. You have built your tightrope from your gold, steel and purple threads and with the help of your network you are hopefully looking at some exciting options. Basing the next decision on just salary is a bad plan. Frederick Herzberg (1923–2000)[4] was a US clinical psychologist who showed that salary can cause discontent, but over a certain level doesn't make you happier. He called it a "hygiene factor". Other hygiene factors include company policy and administration, supervision, working relationships, and status and security. If these are bad we really notice, but once they are good enough other things are more important to us. You might well have experienced some of these (you are reading this book after all). I find fixed-term contracts and toxic relationships cause much of postdoc dissatisfaction. Your next role needs to meet these needs adequately, but is not what is going to set your world on fire (in a good way).

For me Herzberg's "motivational factors" are the ones to look out for and are very related to your purple thread. Factors that are related to you enjoying your time at work and on this planet are:

- achievement
- recognition
- the work itself
- responsibility
- advancement and growth.

The latter is particularly important in relation to salary. You might need to take a dip to get retrained or put through a qualification by a new employer, but in the long run the salary will be higher. That is why it is important to understand the longer-term trajectory possible after your next step, which you can glean from your informational interviews.

Herzberg's theory comes from a time where professional workplaces were very different. The possibilities of remote working and the availability of flexible working could make huge personal differences to you. The latter particularly might help you build a work/life portfolio where each component provides some elements towards your ikigai.

There is an elephant in the room here: you are about to discover that being a postdoc is not so terribly paid. It will be time to do some sums. For all the jobs on the table you need to consider your bottom line (what you need to earn to pay rent in that location and/or commute and cover your other outgoings). Don't forget to look at the wider package – an onsite nursery, gym or subsided canteen could be a real benefit in time as well as money.

I'm often asked what to say if asked about salary at interview or in the following negotiations.

Head to The Leaving Academia Toolkit to explore the practical factors involved in getting the next position. I have hints and tips for interviews and negotiations.

This section has highlighted very deliberately the big thinking we need to do alongside the practicalities we know we must all do to get the next position: search, apply, interview and tell people we are moving on. It is my experience that postdocs who take the time to stop and really think about the next step move on positively and proactively. Importantly they also have seen the value in doing this and so have important tools going forward. The following section looks at what to do once you have moved on. Because your journey doesn't stop there.

ENDNOTES

1. https://marshallgoldsmith.com/book-page-what-got-you-here/ the title of Marshall Goldsmith's book published by Generic 2013
2. Carrying it around like Linus the thumb-sucking kid in the Peanuts cartoon doesn't count.
3. Meaning "really bad" here – a little bit of my Norf London childhood creeping in.
4. A good overview of his two-factor theory is here https://www.simplypsychology.org/herzbergs-two-factor-theory.html

SECTION THREE

SO, YOU'VE GOT YOUR NEW ROLE. WHAT'S NEXT?

You did it. You left academia. You are embarking on that next career step. I hate to break it to you, but I doubt this move will be your last! You may have landed a permanent position, but this may not be your forever home. There are things you will need to do once in the role to ensure you don't just weave another blanket and ensure you move from peak to peak in your career. But don't panic, you have done the big mental heavy lifting by leaving once. You now need to tune into yourself regularly and we will explore how.

Doing something new is hard work. As I write children are returning to the new school year. We are about two weeks in and there are lots of little tired faces trailing their new rucksacks on their walk home past my office window. New rules, friends, expectations and information are all exhausting and not just for little kids. Change we have chosen and strived for can also create unsettling feelings. Don Kelley and Daryl Conner[1] developed a model to understand the emotions we go through when we choose to make a change. Cameron Norton[2] explored this further in relation to changing role.

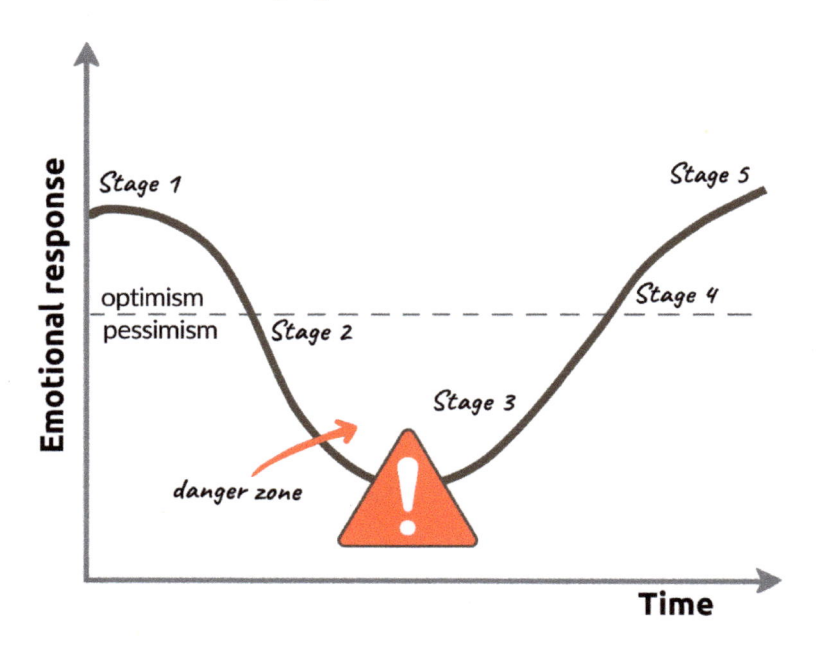

Figure: Emotional response vs Time curve showing Stage 1 (optimism), Stage 2, Stage 3 (danger zone), Stage 4, Stage 5, with a dashed line separating optimism and pessimism.

- Stage 1: Uninformed optimism. You are excited about your role and are focused on doing, rather than thinking.
- Stage 2: Informed pessimism. As you learn more about the new role you realise that you need to learn more and you may identify challenges in your new situation.
- Stage 3: Hopeful realism. You are beginning to understand how the new situation works and can start to identify what you need to succeed.

- Stage 4: Informed optimism. You are settling in and feel more confident having overcome the initial challenges and changes.
- Stage 5: Completion of your personal 'induction' phase. You can now start getting the most out of your new role.

Between stages 2 and 3 we can see a big dip downwards. This is where it is perfectly natural to be asking yourself questions like "Was the change worth it?", "Did I make a mistake?", "Perhaps I should have been content in my last job and not been so ambitious…" Knowing that everyone will experience this to some extent helps. Try to ensure you have a trusted friend or mentor on board to talk to as you settle in. Keep focused on the benefits you saw in taking the new role and give it, and you, some time. How long this takes will be personal but everyone goes through it to some extent.

> *'In every success story you will find someone who has made a courageous decision.'* – Peter F. Drucker

ENDNOTES

1. https://www.mindtools.com/apjsz96/kelley-and-conners-emotional-cycle-of-change
2. https://www.linkedin.com/pulse/what-you-need-know-before-starting-new-job-cameron-norton/

CHAPTER 6: LET'S NOT MAKE ANOTHER BLANKET

My deepest desire is for you to have an amazing career that provides the perfect amount of challenge, impact and personal growth alongside the creature comforts of a good working environment and salary. Coming from a postdoc where you might have spent the past few years switching from project to project and place to place, I understand that you might well want to stay put for several years once you have moved.

Swapping one comfort blanket for the next is, however, worryingly possible. I am reminded of several clergy people I have met whose lives have consisted of attending boarding school, joining the army, teaching at a boarding school and then joining the church. This could be viewed as going from one itchy set of blankets (literally when it comes to boarding school and the army) to the next. Or it could reflect an individual who thrives in highly structured environments. The key difference is thriving not hiding.

The key to thriving is to continue the awareness you needed to build when moving out of academia. Let's revisit the blanket from the perspective of our new role. Our academic blanket was woven from many threads including these weighty ones:

- fears of the unknown – "What else could I do?"; "I don't know if I have the skills"
- sunk cost – "I've spent all this time getting to this point"
- asking the wrong people – "My PI says industry won't suit me"
- vocation – "I have always wanted to be an historian"; "I am a biochemist"
- there is no coming back – "Once you leave, you can't return"

It would be perhaps easy for us to start building a new comfort blanket with new phrases:

- "I don't know if I have those skills"
- "I've spent time getting to grips with my new role"
- "My new boss says I'm doing really well here"
- "I am still using my history/biochemistry skills"
- "I'm getting further away from who I was"

This chapter highlights three ways of keeping your threads in tightrope mode rather than weaving another blanket.

The day one question

I had landed a training team management job at the ancient (make of that what you will) University of Cambridge. I'd made a pot of coffee and took my steaming mug down from *my* office (yes, a whole room just for me!) to my boss's for my first meeting. Her first question floored me:

So, what is your next career move?

"Hang on", I thought, "I haven't started this one yet!" Once over the shock, she explained that I needed to use that as a focus for developing myself and building experiences during my time in this role.

This brought up two points that really hit home. The first was this role is not forever which is a tough thing to face. I felt as if I'd just scaled a cliff to get the job with my grappling hook, and now, I look up and discover I'm only sitting on a ridge? I confess to feeling a little exhausted at that point! But tied to that there was a sense of liberation. If this role isn't forever, that means I have future opportunities and choices. This is not the endgame of my career. It is the opening move from this point.

The second was "I am not defined by this role but I will be transformed by it". I have the chance to learn new skills and to try out new experiences. Those will certainly add to my CV. But there is a bigger picture here in that I would be a different person in a year, eighteen months.[1] My choices of focus and attention would determine what sort of stepping stone this role might be. I went back to my office and started looking at training courses (a natural place to start when you are in my business!).

When starting a new role there will always be things you don't know how to do (otherwise where is the stretch?) and these will necessarily need your focus to start with. If we think about that change curve there are bound to be some gaps identified in stages one to three as you settle in and really understand your role. Mastering these will certainly help you with your career as you want to be successful in your role.

But the day one question does demand that our eyes look out to a further horizon. It is important to do on day one because that is the time to harness your excitement at your new role and dream of the possibilities it could give you, before we hit stages two and three of the curve in the last chapter. I would encourage you to reflect on and write down the answers to the following:[2]

1. What would be an exciting next step?
2. What would you love to learn/experience in this role that moves you in that direction?
3. How can you make this happen?

Another thread (the tripwire)

When working with postdocs on moving out of academia, a surprisingly common question is "What if I hate it?" If you have followed the ideas in the preceding chapters you have ended up somewhere that you thought you would enjoy, and played to your three threads of steel, purple and gold. We should make thought-out rational decisions based on the best information we can get at the time.

But there is the possibility we might have chosen wrongly. In their book *Decisive* Chip and Dan Heath[3] set out their WRAP framework as a process for making decisions big and small. The P is perhaps surprising but necessary: "Prepare to be wrong". We are back to the awareness piece here. If we don't set aside a time to ask ourselves "how's it going?", we might be en route for a Plateau or Plummet without realising it. Sometimes it might be obvious we have made the wrong choice, but in general we need to set a tripwire.

We've all seen the movies with the incredibly thin, almost invisible thread that the villain fails to see, snags, and then all manner of spotlights and weaponry are trained upon them. We need to lay down this delicate thread pretty much on day one so the spotlights illuminate our situation at the right time (no weapons required). For setting up a tripwire, we need a specific criterion or event that, when met or crossed, triggers a re-evaluation of our current situation.

Most workplaces offer scheduled six- or twelve-month performance reviews. If you haven't received any promotions, raises, or significant new opportunities by that milestone (assuming you're performing well and exceeding expectations), it might serve as a signal to reconsider your options. Another tripwire could be more personal; for example, if you find yourself consistently dreading work for an extended period, say two weeks, then that emotional state serves as your tripwire to reassess your position and explore your options.

However, if we have just started a role then timing for the tripwire is very important. Too long into your contract and you might find things needed addressing sooner. But we need to be mindful not to ask "how's it going?" when in stages two and three of the change curve. It could be too easy to view a natural, unsettled feeling as the ringing of alarm bells. The figure of three months feels a good compromise here. Put it into your diary on day one. Your new workplace might offer an induction or probation process which could dovetail nicely into your personal tripwire.

Setting a tripwire helps you avoid drifting along in a job that may not be the best fit for you. It creates a predetermined point of reflection, so you can more objectively evaluate how things are going and make a more informed decision about whether to stay or seek other opportunities. If you are great at reflection and self-accountability you may well just need to set some time in your diary. Personally I know that these reflections are much better for me if they are done with a trusted friend or coach who can act as a critical guide. There is clarity in a conversation where you can receive challenge ("What aren't you telling me?") and support ("Sounds like you are making great progress.").

Here are some questions you might ask yourself (or get that coaching buddy to ask) three months into a new job to assess whether you're in the right place:

1. Can I grow in multiple dimensions (skill set, network, career ladder) here?
2. Are my initial expectations about the job met or disproved?
3. What feedback have I received, and how does it align with my self-assessment?
4. Have I seen any red flags or cultural misalignments that I initially overlooked?
5. How do I feel about the job when I am not in the workplace?
6. What indicators will tell me it's time to reassess my position here?

They are suggested here as starting points to uncover your thoughts. Whether positive or negative, these thoughts need to be turned into an action plan. If they are negative, it may mean moving on or changing things, but you know you can do this now. If positive, you need to chart a route to maximise this role.

You're not a cat. Be curious.

"Curiosity killed the cat"[4] is an odd English phrase usually used to warn against asking questions. It carries the connotation that the asker would be detrimentally affected if the answer were revealed. I have yet to meet a feline postdoc (I think cats would go straight for the vice-chancellor type jobs), and so you, my friend, need to deploy that curiosity now you are in your new role.

When you were in academia you knew the academic routes forward and hopefully this book has helped you chart the myriad of non-academic adventures you could have starting from Planet Postdoc. Your new position has now opened up another set of possibilities going forward. There are now roles on your radar that were either out of reach because you needed to take the intermediate step or that were simply invisible where you started.

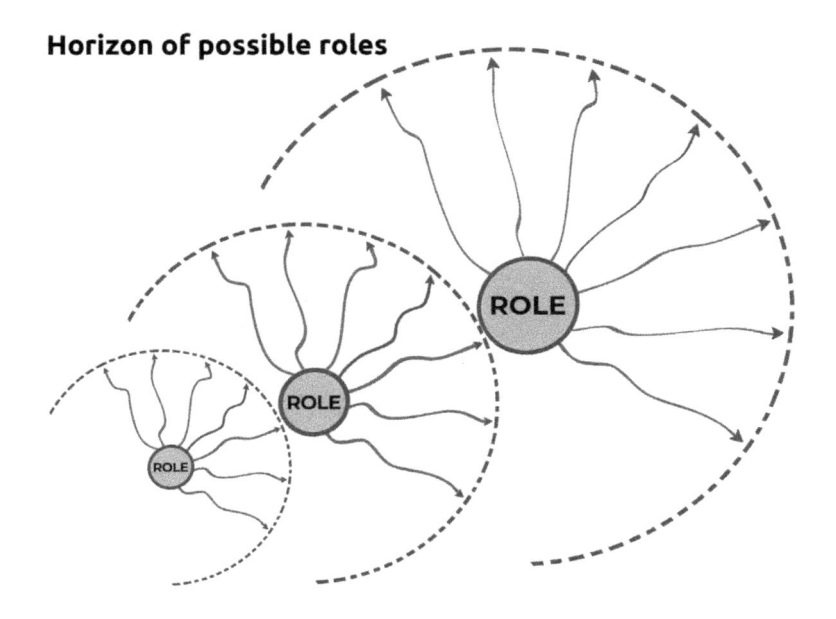

Horizon of possible roles

It is time to get curious about these other roles, especially if you have just landed your first job in the "outside world". If you are working for a big corporate, there will be whole divisions who do things you hadn't even thought of.

In smaller companies and start-ups those things might be just one of the hats your colleagues have to wear. Marketing, product design, compliance, finance, logistics, operations all might be a mystery to you at this point, but they might be hiding your next step. Broadening your horizons internally could be as easy as having a cuppa with someone, working on cross company projects or joining the company's five-a-side/quiz/charity team. Cultivate curiosity and ask other people about their roles to help you understand your new organisation better. Being genuinely interested in others' perspectives will make you a more effective communicator and collaborator.

As a former postdoc one of the things that is most attractive about you to the wider world is your ability to think, analyse and create. To completely misquote Yoda: "Curiosity leads to creativity. Creativity leads to innovation. Innovation leads to thought leadership. I sense much leadership potential in you." Curiosity about industry trends, policy advancements and what your network is doing coupled with a powerful critical thinking engine (your brain) has the potential to create opportunities for your new organisation and you.

Demonstrating a willingness to learn and adapt makes you more valuable to an employer, opening doors to new opportunities. In today's rapidly changing work environment, the ability to learn and adapt is more valuable than ever. As I write, Artificial Intelligence (AI) is the latest saviour/scare factor for all our jobs. During the pandemic, I could help many of my clients get up to speed as I'd been using Zoom for several years. Sharing knowledge through teaching or mentoring is both personally and professionally rewarding. But to do that we need to keep up with new publications, attend webinars and take short courses.

Another fascinating way of learning is through "reverse mentoring" where you might pair up with a younger colleague to learn from each other. I'm mentioning it because it might be an unusual thought that you are not necessarily the youngest/most junior in the team. However, those junior colleagues may have been with the company longer or have just emerged from a very up-to-date degree.

Even though you're out of academia, the learning should never stop! But then I don't think you wanted it to.

Please take 5 minutes to leave me a review, it helps other people to decide if they want to read the book, and I'll be eternally grateful. If you're reading on Kindle just scroll to the end of the book. If you're reading the paperback, please go to your favourite bookstore.

Remember, you can get the promised downloads at www.thenerdcoach.co.uk/leaving_academia or scan the QR code.

ENDNOTES

1. And I certainly was! Eighteen months saw me embark on my freelance adventure. Perhaps I'll save that time for my autobiography.
2. In fact sending yourself a scheduled email for three months' time might be perfect given the next section! A great tool for this is https://www.futureme.org
3. Chip and Dan Heath *Decisive: How to Make Better Choices in Life and Work* 2013 Random House Business
4. The original version of the words was "care killed the cat." ("Care" meant concern or worry.) William Shakespeare used the phrase in *Much Ado About Nothing*, written around 1598.

CHAPTER 7:
PEAK TO PEAK: THE NEXT CAREER STEPS

This book has been about moving out of academia, but it does also provide a road map for taking the next step. And the next. What is exciting and perhaps a little scary is that very few of us have these mapped out. We do not know how long we will stay in one role or what the next step might be.

Yesterday I was at a postdoc event and was asked, "Physics? So how did you get here?" I was surrounded by genome scientists, but the question was about my career track not my lack of biology. If I look at my starting point (degree in physics) to where I am now (author/coach/speaker) then it is certainly a quantum leap. However, each step at the time seemed a logical opportunity to take. Importantly each step built on and used skills and experiences from across all the previous steps not just the last one.

Take inspiration from the careers of people doing something interesting. Start by looking at trajectories from the top down (that is an interesting role; how did they start?)

or from the bottom up (here are a selection of ex-postdocs in my field; where did they go?). The journey will not necessarily be a linear trajectory regarding salary, responsibility, technical challenge or happiness. Sometimes we might take a wrong turn for all the right reasons; this book should give you some helpful prompts along the way.

One to many: building your career a peak at a time

Let's revisit the Postdoc Peak, Plateau and Plummet model for a moment. If we combine this model with the idea of a tripwire from the previous chapter, we can consciously create check-in and reflection points along our career journey. I've outlined these on the diagram as vertical bars.

- Check-in one shows someone still "on the up" still gaining skills and experiences.
- Check-in two is at the tipping point. We need to design our tripwires to capture any signs of slow down. Quantitative questions could be helpful here.
- Check-in three shows two possibilities – a "meh" dissatisfaction and a starting to get miserable face. They both need to be avoided which is why we need regular check-ins!

Many workplaces offer annual appraisals or reviews which can be a helpful check-in with your boss but to my mind annually is too infrequent. I suggest a simple check-in could be done monthly and perhaps a longer one every quarter. And not just when you are new to the role – we want to avoid the blanket weaving danger zone too! Some of my steps were too late, so would have really benefited from this approach.

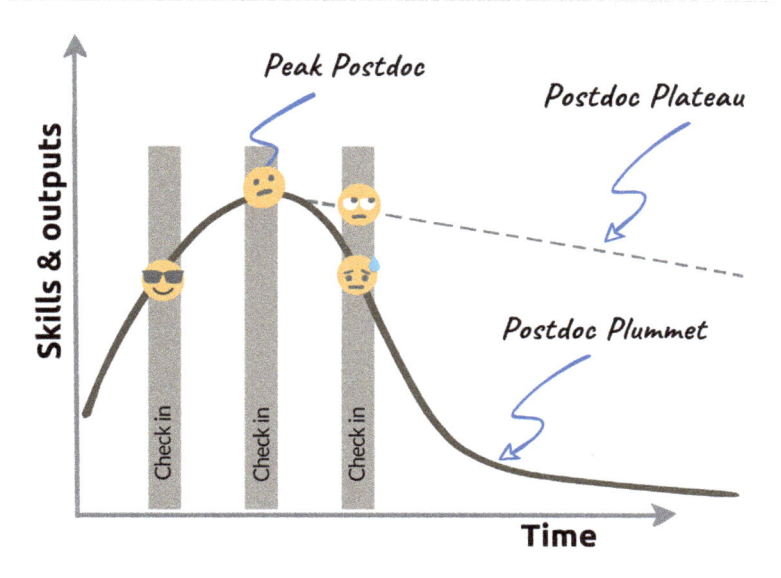

Figure: A graph with "Skills & outputs" on the y-axis and "Time" on the x-axis. A curve rises to "Peak Postdoc" then either continues as "Postdoc Plateau" (dashed line) or declines as "Postdoc Plummet". Three vertical bars labelled "Check in" are shown along the curve with emoji faces.

But this will not happen unless we build it into our diaries. Since it is easy to deprioritise ourselves in busy workplaces I suggest the idea of habit stacking that James Clear talks about in his book *Atomic Habits*.[1] Can we tag our review onto something that happens each month? It could be something technical (as a postdoc I had a regular nitrogen fill of a magnet), a recurring meeting or even payday (a payslip would be a good reminder!).

The worst career decisions are those we take on autopilot. I call these travelator decisions. A travelator is one of those flat escalators in airports where in theory you can walk along slightly faster than those on either side. They are usually arranged in a chain. Walk along, step off, take a couple of steps, onto the next one, stretching the length of the terminal. Very easy to go from one to the next – just looking ahead to the next obvious step. But the gaps in between are departure gates. If we pause at the gaps we could escape to Tahiti or the Maldives but only if we stop to read the destinations.

This is how postdocs can get stuck in successive contracts with their eyes firmly fixed on academia ahead. But that sort of thinking can happen anywhere. When a management position appeared in front of me when my boss left, I jumped on that next track without stopping to think, to assess my options or even to double-check it was really for me. It really wasn't. I learnt a lot in the following eighteen months but I was much more careful to look at all my possible options when I decided to leave.

Chapter 7: Peak to peak: the next career steps 89

I think an ideal career trajectory should see us leaping from role to role at the peak. The exact alignment of new opportunity meets peak role satisfaction might not be completely possible but we can increase our chances by being on the lookout for opportunities, understanding where we are in our current role and maintaining that curious mindset that got you into research in the first place.

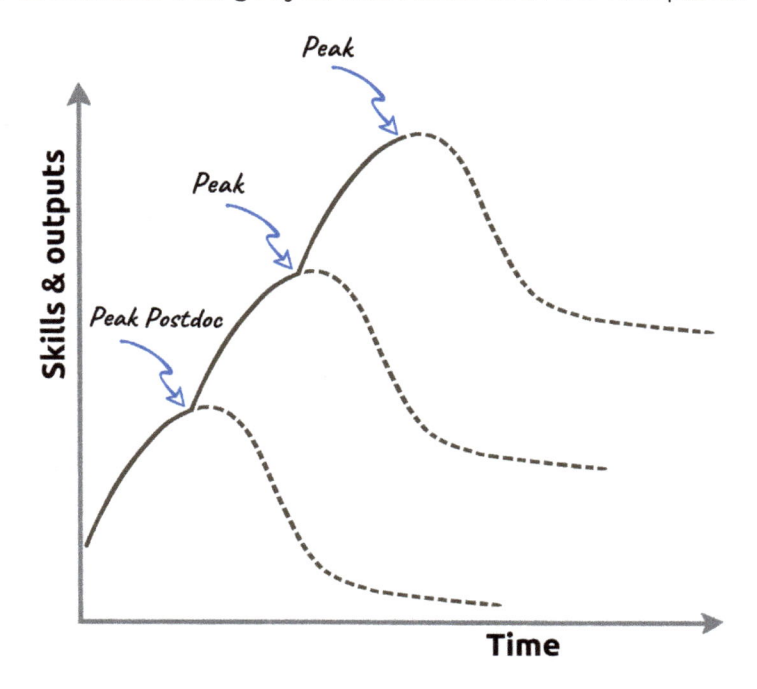

Figure: Skills & outputs vs Time, showing successive overlapping curves with labels "Peak Postdoc", "Peak", and "Peak".

Postdoc D "Beginning my journey in psychology, cognitive science and behavioural genetics, I eventually found myself in a postdoc position at a large pharma company. It felt like I had the best of both worlds, where I could pursue my research questions akin to academia while also enjoying the stability offered by the industry. A one-year contract in the U.S. eventually led to a permanent position, a decision that I found to be pragmatic. In industry, you're not constantly searching for your next job; instead, you have the opportunity to conduct meaningful research. While there's stress and a focus on reputation, publishing remains important, albeit with high standards and a preference for high-impact factor journals. The work leans towards more managerial roles, shifting away from the bench, making it difficult to compare directly with academia. One key difference is the potentially reduced flexibility and the need to be cautious about what you can share when working for a large pharmaceutical company.

Having experienced both academia and industry through two postdocs and a position in large pharma, I realised that my academic career might not have the room for progression that I desired. The academic landscape often felt like a leaking pipeline, especially with a noticeable absence of female leaders, particularly in regions like Italy where I began my journey. In an academic institution, there was no clear career path forward, which led me to seek stability in industry. In industry, it's all about working as a team to make improvements together, quite different from the sometimes tricky dynamics of academic presentations.

Transitioning from academia to industry meant taking on more responsibility. In industry, you're accountable for your actions and goals, with a focus on metrics and achieving them. The postdoc life demanded hard work, but industry introduced a clearer structure with intermediate goals, allowing me to track progress more easily. I realised that in a global company, I had more opportunities to apply for proper jobs, not just postdocs. The journey taught me that the more you know, the more you realise you don't know, encouraging me to explore new boundaries.

I also noticed differences across regions. The UK appeared more open to a variety of backgrounds, whereas continental Europe, like Italy, could pose challenges when returning to work after a career break. In northern Europe, such hurdles seemed less significant, and forging collaborations with a focus on leveraging my skills and degree background became key to my professional growth."

Stay connected. Not tethered

Robin Dunbar a British anthropologist is famous for his "Dunbar number"; on average humans can sustain 150 meaningful contacts at any one point.[2] Of those we have five "loved ones" and fifteen "close friends". What is often missed out is that he also suggests we have around 1,500 "people you recognise". As we move through our careers, we will weave a wide net of people we have worked with and alongside. You can't (and probably don't want to) promote them all to "loved one" status. So, what should we do?

Starting at the beginning when we are looking to leave our role, we must endeavour at all costs not to burn our bridges.[3] This means working hard on those difficult conversations, understanding the situations of the people around us and ensuring a fair and equitable transition or handover as you depart as we discussed in chapter 4. The world is too small a place to make "enemies". People may not understand our decision to leave but we can strive to leave amicably. It then might be worth checking you have a way to keep in contact should you want to. I absolutely understand that some people we may just want to relegate to the past.

Currently it is very easy to be "connected" through LinkedIn or similar. That is not the same as maintaining a connection. But we can't possibly have a conversation with everyone each week. The following are some low-cost (in time and effort) methods to keep being one of those people your contacts "recognise". They will also serve to inform those who might be looking to work with you in the future.

- Post updates on LinkedIn (or similar) that let people know what you are up to, your successes and events attended. Choose a frequency you can sustain.
- Be mindful of the information that comes your way. Who would find this paper/event/group interesting? Send them a brief friendly note along with the information.

- Reciprocate with your network. Comment on their posts meaningfully (not just a reaction such as a like). Again, choose an amount of time you can sustain as an investment.

Connection is great but as we chart our own career paths we need to be mindful of the labels and attitudes that may hold us back. I am sure I might well be still mentally labelled as X's postdoc by some of my research connections. If this is just a quick aide memoire, fine but if it is pigeonholing[4] us then it doesn't help people to see who we have become. This labelling can cut both ways.

The first is that our former colleagues can't see us as the people we are now. This is another great reason for reminding our network what we are up to now. There is a small subset of people who have decided at some point what you are and what you aren't and their view stays fixed. They may even tell you! We have permission to question these labels and reject them. That may seem obvious but might require some mental heavy lifting if it is someone whose opinion we have respected in the past. To paraphrase Tara Mohr and Gay Hendricks[5] again:

We cannot control what someone else will think about our career. We are responsible for our own career.

The second is more dangerous. We may label ourselves based on our prior experiences. If our previous role has only let us express our analytical side then it may be hard to convince ourselves we are anything but analytical. I think as researchers our disciplines have done much to define our mindsets with their teaching and problem-solving methods. It took me a long time to reconcile my creative and intuitive skills with my vision of what a physicist looked like. I was once asked, "Were you this creative when you were in research?" Sadly no. You need to give yourself time to explore who you are now in your new role as opposed to who you were (or the labels associated with that) before.

Both of these can be unhelpful tethers to the past. We tether things with rope to stop them escaping the bounds we have defined for them: a tent is tethered to stop it blowing away, a goat is tethered to stop it eating the flowers. If we are to walk that strong three-thread tightrope into our careers we need to make sure we aren't tied to the starting point, preventing us from reaching the next peak. And the next.

> Postdoc E "Starting my Ph.D., I didn't have a clear five-year plan, and academia wasn't my ultimate goal, but I was passionate about research. I wanted to ensure that I wasn't leaving academia because I thought I couldn't make it, so I pursued a postdoc. This decision allowed me to be more intentional in my career choices and gave me a second chance at research. While I loved many aspects of the postdoc experience, the academic career path felt like a never-ending treadmill, and it didn't align with my interests.

I was about 90% sure that academia wasn't for me, but I decided to use the postdoc as an opportunity to explore other options. I became deeply interested in consulting and entrepreneurship, enjoyed networking events, and engaged with policy networks.

I realised that not every job needed to follow a linear path, and my decisions were about learning and expanding my CV. In academia we can be easily labelled and it defines our identity. Whereas I was approaching each role with the attitude that it doesn't have to define me, I just have to grow there. I valued learning about diverse fields, such as drug development, and always approached networking with curiosity.

As time has passed, I feel I am becoming less of an expert but my increased exposure to industry means there are more intersections and possibilities. I have also stepped into highlighting my softer skills on my CV such as international background, being emotionally intelligent and my forward-looking approach having moved around the sector."

ENDNOTES

1. https://jamesclear.com/atomic-habits James Clear *Atomic Habits* 2021 Generic
2. Robin Dunbar *How Many Friends Does One Person Need? Dunbar's Number and Other Evolutionary Quirks* 2010 Faber
3. "Magrat plunged on with the brave desperation of someone dancing in the light of their burning bridges." Is one of my favourite Terry Pratchett quotes. *Witches Abroad* 1992 Corgi Books
4. I used to get my post in a small wooden pigeonhole at my college. Only little letters would fit. Typically, pigeonholing means to put someone into a restrictive category or type.
5. Tara Mohr *Playing Big* 2015 3rd edition Arrow and Gay Hendrick *The Big Leap* 2010 HarperOne

CONCLUSION: PROVE IT'S POSSIBLE

My sincere hope is that not only have you found this book helpful but that you are about to embark on the next amazing chapter of your career. You now have tools to leave academia unless of course you decided to stay in a positive and deliberate way. Even better, these can be applied to those future career steps that you can see ahead and those that have yet to be unveiled in your future.

My longer-term dream, which I doubt will please my publisher, is that perhaps this specific title might be obsolete in a few years' time. Why? Because I hope as careers become increasingly squiggly and wonderfully complex we won't have silos of choice. The career for life is for a previous generation – my parents' one. My generation will hopefully break the mould of seeing academia separate from other areas that add value culturally, socially and economically. I don't want to pull down the ivory towers but rather see sky bridges from pinnacles in industry, policy, charity and education moving our society collectively forward. And along those bridges will be people moving freely. Not judged by type of background or nominal status but by the value and impact that their skills and experiences bring. There will be less of a focus on leaving and more on arriving. I know it is a lofty ideal. I have a strong steel thread of optimism.

Me? A mentor?

You can move us toward that dream. If you have moved on from academia, don't just become "that person who moved on". Keep in contact and let people know what is possible. To continue the threads metaphor – let down a rope ladder and hold it steady so other postdocs and PhD students can explore the landscape and make informed career decisions. What do you wish you had known at the start of this career leap? Write it down and then share it.

Many universities have formal mentoring schemes and alumni networks that do just this. Don't wait to be asked – get involved! And if you don't like formal structures then pop back for a chat or send a friendly email.

Dr Seuss wrote a great poem called *The Places You'll Go*[1]. It is often used for commencement speeches and seems very appropriate at this point:

> *Out there things can happen*
> *and frequently do*
> *to people as brainy*
> *and footsy as you.*
> *And then things start to happen,*
> *don't worry. Don't stew.*
> *Just go right along.*
> *You'll start happening too.*

Dr Seuss

Let me know where you go,
Emma

ENDNOTES

1. *Oh, The Places You'll Go*, Dr Seuss, 1990 Random House

ABOUT THE AUTHOR

Dr. Emma Williams finds herself wondering if she has in fact left academia or not. Having spent the past 30 plus years in and around universities, a case could be made that she loves the complex and slightly bonkers environment.

Her journey started as a physics student at the University of Cambridge moving into medical physics for a PhD and postdoc. She has been there and worn the lab coat/scrubs. Despite doing research being her nerdy childhood ambition, after 3 years of postdoc she realised she was ready for pastures new. This would not have happened without a good chunk of reflection time. Admittedly it was enforced – never break your leg when 7 months pregnant. But she encourages review and reflection in all the researchers she works with, without the necessity for injury.

Her first move from academic research was into the professional services side of university. Working to support researchers whilst gazing into the inner workings of a university was fascinating. Designing and delivering training employed her previous skills and experiences whilst stretching into new areas. However there followed a self-confessed travelator career decision to take a management position. Her fantastic team were out doing the fun stuff (training and coaching) whilst committees and paperwork beckoned on her desk. Her tripwire moment came in the middle of one of those dreadful meetings. The presenter stated that "We come to work because we enjoy it". Lightbulb. She didn't.

The next move was very much more informed and used many of the techniques talked about in this book. She stepped out of the comfort blankets of the university system and a steady pay packet for the uncharted lands of being self-employed. This environment with its highs, lows and amazing autonomy has allowed her purple, steel and gold threads to develop and intertwine. Being a business owner has opened out the uncharted lands of consultant, coach, speaker, and author. The latter two would have astounded her postdoc self. The possibilities, twists and turns that careers can take makes her work with postdocs exciting and challenging.

This is Emma's third book[1] following on from *What Every Postdoc Needs to Know* written with Drs Elvidge and Spencely in 2017 and *The UNIque Guide for Women: Confidently embracing your career in research and beyond* in 2023. Works in the pipeline include a children's book with Dr Jo Montgomery and a guide for those researchers looking to move into the financial sector.

When not working Emma can be found shooting her recurve bow, tackling jigsaws and immersing herself in sci fi and fantasy books and films. She brings creativity, empathy and usually a large coffee to all her endeavours.

Head to https://thenerdcoach.co.uk/ to find out more.

ENDNOTES

1. She can be heard muttering "See my collected works" like Gilderoy Lockhart in JK Rowling's *Harry Potter and the Chamber of Secrets* Bloomsbury 1998

ACKNOWLEDGEMENTS

Both my academic journey and my business journey start with my Dad, Roy Thompson. I have fond memories of sitting down with a chemistry set with him. Later on, I would tick off invoices and change price stickers in his pharmacy shop eventually working as a dispensary assistant. I was surrounded by entrepreneurial lessons which I appreciate more and more. Thanks Dad.

To the hundreds, possibly thousands, of researchers who I have had the pleasure to work with: you are the shoulders of giants that this book stands on. Your stories, CVs and discussions are helping a new generation of researchers. Particular thanks to my "one reader" and those whose interviews contributed to the book.

My book writing team has made all the difference between file on my computer and book out into the world. Thank you to my book buddies for their thoughtful feedback and to those who have endorsed the book. Thanks to Debs Jenkins who yet again has nursed a book into being and placed me into the perfect writing cohort for this adventure. The support, accountability, laughter and tears I have shared with Finola Howard, Rachel

Evers and Sally Murphy during the writing process have been magical. I have learnt so much from yourselves and your books but am still working on my Irish accent. Thanks also to Susannah Simmons and Dan Kowalski as the cohort who went before. Thanks also to Lisa de Caux who must be the funniest editor in the world. If this book has a cover, it will be down to Jayr Cuario being infinitely patient and flexible.

Your support network is everything in life and mine is awesome. Thank you to my household nerds for the coffee and listening to the sentences I tried out on them: Richard and our boys, Ben, Alex and Bisto. If you become those you surround yourself with then I am on to a good thing with Ginette, Jo, Karen, Kate, Kirsty, Nicola, Rowena and Sarah. It is my round for sure. And because you should seek feedback far and wide, thanks to Frodo and Pippin the house rabbits who nibbled early drafts.

OTHER BOOKS BY DR EMMA WILLIAMS

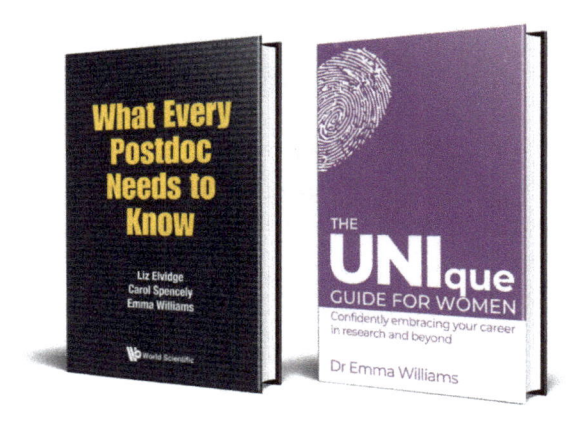

Get Dr Emma Williams' other books at

What Every Postdoc Needs to Know:
www.worldscientific.com
The UNIque Guide for Women:
https://womenresearchers.com/unique/

MORE PRAISE FOR LEAVING ACADEMIA

Well-written and thought-provoking, this book reminds us of the real-world value that we have as researchers. Full of insightful anecdotes and reflective prompts, Williams encourages us to think beyond the obvious and challenge our career expectations to consider what we truly want to pursue, and why. A recommended read for everyone, whether you want to stay in academia or not!

Simone Eizagirre, PhD student, Physics

The book is very concise and gives a great summary of postdoc journey. It also gives postdocs courage to jump to industry.

Dr Liu Shi, Assoc Director of Bioinformatics
& Biomarkers, Sosei Heptares

Leaving academia is no easy feat. Even if it's something that deep down you know is the right decision for you, making the leap can feel daunting and isolating, especially after investing so much time and energy into your academic career. Emma perfectly captures the challenges that come with making the big jump to a non-academic career, whilst providing tangible advice for how to navigate the entire process, from considering the decision to leave, to landing your next role. My wish would be for a book like this to be made available to all final year PhD researchers, whether they want to stay or move onto new opportunities outside of academia.

Dr Danielle Perro,
Women's Health Researcher & Science Communicator

Forget dusty dissertations and tenure tantrums! Emma Williams' "Leaving Academia" is your sassy best friend, spilling the tea on academia's underbelly and cheering you on with a margarita in hand! Her advice is like sunshine on a rainy day – it warms your soul and makes you want to skip to your next chapter.

It's like she's whispering secrets of freedom directly into your ear, secrets that will have you ditching the safety blanket and booking a one-way ticket to your wildest dreams. The visuals are a game-changer, especially the clever 'peak to peak' concept. It's like Emma's right there with you, cheering you on as you plot your next big move. So, ditch the drudgery, grab this book and get ready to launch yourself into a future that's brighter than a unicorn's horn!

Debbie Jenkins, The Asset Path

Leaving Academia' is an informative book inspiring to take action. It is written in an engaging style which made me feel like having a conversation with the author who is supportive, re-assuring and pragmatic.

The book provides lots of practical tips and exercises as well as links to further information for and beyond the move away from academia. Interwoven with examples which cover a range of experiences, it is something to hold onto even after having made the transition.

My suggestion is to read it from start to end to envision how your journey may unfold and then return to the beginning to go through the chapters one by one and follow up with actions. The author is right there to guide you along.

Dr Anke Husmann, Wellcome Sanger Institute

Like its author, and everything she creates, This book is fabulous. In my opinion it isn't just for people considering leaving 'planet postdoc'. It is an insightful guide and practical resource for anyone considering leaving a profession that they have dedicated years of their life to. Emma has an engaging writing style and her use of humour and graphics takes it to another level. I loved the theme of the blanket and the threads that are woven (pun intended) throughout the book. Highly recommended!

Susannah Simmons, Multi-Passionate Entrepreneur

I really enjoy reading this book. I think my friends and postdoc colleagues would enjoy it too. I'm currently doing research at the University of Oxford and I'm thinking about my future career. This book talks about the real experiences of postdocs, which I can relate to. It shows the difficult parts of academic life that aren't always talked about, even at prestigious universities like Oxford. It's important for students and new researchers to know what academic life is really like, and this book does a good job of showing that.

Dr. Ping Lu, PostDoctoral Researcher,
Institute of Biomedical Engineering, University of Oxford

Reading Leaving Academia is like sitting down with that tactful friend who will kindly challenge you by asking all the right questions, even if you're mildly anxious about them doing so. It's not taboo to explore leaving academia – postdocs have the most incredible skill sets and proven assets in a wealth of roles beyond academic research – and Emma's warm and supportive tone helps ease anxieties and inspire rational pro-active thinking.

This short book certainly packs that soft punch; imploring busy Postdoc warriors to apply the same level of curiosity and planning to their career journey as they do their research projects. It also provides a wealth of resources and exercises to support Postdocs in building the evidence-base needed to inform their decisions about which exciting and fulfilling boarding gates they should head to next...

Leaving Academia is sure to be a short but highly impactful read for all postdocs!

Dr Diane Swallow, Postdoc Programme Lead,
Wellcome Sanger Institute

I have never read a book before where I have felt so relatable to. For a moment, I even thought Emma had somehow managed to sneak into my thoughts and put them down into words. I highly recommend any PhD students and Postdocs to have a read. In this wonderful book, you will get a chance to learn that it is ok to be unsure about the future, but coming outside of your comfort zone will bring you many other exciting opportunities.

(soon to be Dr) Irene Villar Rodriguez, PhD Student
at London Centre for Nanotechnology, UCL

Leaving Academia" is a brilliant, clever and insightful book packed with the best advice ever if you are considering leaving academia for pastures new. With an approachable and engaging tone, inspiring courage and offering a clear call to action, Dr. Emma's three decades of expertise in higher education and research is distilled into a powerful guide for navigating the postdoctoral career transition. Through encounters with hundreds of postdoctoral researchers—her 'Sams'—Dr. Emma has crafted a narrative that is as much a personal journey as it is a universal guide. Her priceless insights and deep engagement with the academic community underscore a heartfelt commitment to aiding researchers' growth and transition. The book emerges not just as a roadmap but as a comforting companion through the often solitary journey of leaving academia.

Dr. Emma's unique blend of humour and wisdom transforms daunting challenges into manageable steps, making the journey toward a new career path less intimidating and more of a shared adventure. Her personal anecdotes, brilliant metaphors and practical advice resonate deeply, offering readers not only strategies for resilience and adaptability but also the reassurance that they are not alone.

This book is essential for anyone at an academic crossroads—postdoctoral researchers, career advisors, mentors, and anyone who supports researchers through transformative phases.

Rachel Evers, Deputy General Counsel,
World Food Programme

Should I stay or should I go? Choosing to leave academia can be hard, but Emma's book takes you by the hand and helps you answer the many questions and feelings associated with making this decision. This book is the toolkit you need to enable you to take stock and reflect on what you want from your career, identify the skills that you have and set you on the path to your new role! If you have ever had the niggling question "What next?!?" in the back of your mind, then I encourage you to read this book!

Dr Karen Hinxman,
Head of the White Rose University Consortium

Emma writes with a stroke of genius, offering her readers a breath of fresh air with each sentence and the delight of relatable characters who create a hum of resonance. This book is essential reading for our times. In a certainly scary world, we can be afraid to leave our comfort zone and strike out on our own hero's journey. But in doing so, we miss out on the chance to experience an epic adventure with a holy grail that surely deserves a good go. Read this book and come to your own conclusion, I suspect that like me, you will conclude that ignoring the itch would only be rash.

Sally Murphy, Business Storyteller

This is a book that will act as a champion for your future self in ways that are both pragmatic and powerful. Dr Emma Williams shows us that preparation brings power with practical examples of that in action. She reassures us that it's "okay to pursue you" and I love that we unravel as we weave each version of ourselves using our three threads of values, strengths and courage. I can see the future she proposes of people moving fluidly, judged only by the value their skills and experiences bring and that our arrival is not at the expense of our leaving. This book is wise and filled with a consciousness that can only be revealed in the simplicity of truly understanding what matters. Yoda comes to mind immediately!

Finola Howard,
Marketing & Brand Positioning Strategist